Who Was Jack The Stripper?

The Hammersmith Nudes' Murders

By Neil Milkins

Steve Thomas
Design And Print
01495 726220

stevethomasdesign@gmail.com

First published in April 2011

ISBN 978-0-9568512-0-8

British Library Cataloguing in Publication Data: a record for this book is available from the British Library.

In accord with British law, a copy of this publication has been placed as a legal deposit with each of the following: The British Library's Legal Deposit Office – The Bodleian Library of the University of Oxford – Cambridge University Library – The National Library of Scotland – The Library of Trinity College, Dublin – The National Library of Wales.

Published, sold and distributed by
Rose Heyworth Press,
67 Arael View, Abertillery, Gwent, NP13 1SU.
Tel - 01495 213744
Email - n.milkin@sky.com

Page/cover, design and layout © Steve Thomas.
stevethomasdesign@gmail.com
Tel: 01495 726220 - 07850 074276

Who Was Jack The Stripper?

Contents

FOREWORD

Neil Milkins has produced a thorough and well-researched book – with much of that primary research stemming from the National Archives at Kew – and as a consequence he shines new light on the Hammersmith Nudes' Murders.

Inevitably, attention will be drawn to the suspect that he names for these serial killings, but I for one was equally impressed by the way that Milkins carefully reconstructed the lives of the women that were murdered.

As such I read this book as a welcome antidote to [the late David Seabrook's book] 'Jack of Jumps' in which these women were pathologised, denigrated, and almost blamed for their own untimely deaths.

Professor David Wilson,
Centre for Applied Criminology,
Birmingham City University.

Professor Wilson is Britain's leading criminologist who regularly appears on Sky, BBC and ITV news, and in national newspapers such as The Daily Mail and The Guardian. He is a broadcaster and has presented many television documentaries. He presented four series of 'The Crime Squad' for BBC1, and also 'Leave No Trace' and 'Too Young to Die?' which discussed the plight of young people on death row in the USA. He is also the author of more than fifteen books, the latest being 'The Lost British Serial Killer – Closing the Case on Peter Tobin and Bible John', published in 2010 by Sphere. Scotsman, Robbie Coltrane OBE is the actor well known for his role as Dr Eddie Fitzgerald in the television psychological thriller, "Cracker." Himself a Scot, Professor David Wilson is the real-life "Cracker." Prior to taking up his academic post, Professor Wilson was a prison governor. He worked at Grendon, Wormwood Scrubs and at Woodhill in Milton Keynes – where he designed and ran the two units for the twelve most violent prisoners in the country. This brought him into contact with some of the most fearsome felons of recent times, including serial killer Dennis Nilsen.

DEDICATION

This book is dedicated to Gillian Kirk, for her tireless efforts while helping to research for this book. She has provided numerous important photographs of her father, former West Middlesex Coroner Dr Harold George Broadbridge and his coroner's officers and pathologists.

Gillian has also provided an invaluable proofreading and copy-editing service. When the author almost gave up trying to get this book published, she wouldn't. Bravo Gillian!

INTRODUCTION

During the *"Swinging Sixties"* hordes of the easily impressed descended on London to tread the streets *"paved with gold."* The glitz and glamour unfortunately was reserved for only a minority. A minority like modelling icons Twiggy and Jean Shrimpton and photographers David Bailey and Terence Donovan. These four actually helped create *"Swinging London,"* a culture of high fashion and celebrity chic. London in the sixties flaunted absurd and unforgettable fashion, the most memorable being the mini-skirt. New musical styles were created which led to flower power, civil rights marches and so-called sexual freedom. A sunny optimism permeated everything and the possibilities seemed endless. But, like the pot of gold at the end of the rainbow, it was all just an illusion.

On the other side of the coin was the sad reality. For many, beneath the glitz and glamour lay the stark truth. Some had left home to escape an unhappy home life only to be trapped in a downward spiral of hopelessness through drink, drugs, prostitution and vagrancy. For many who survived, looking back to the era of the sixties was not a happy experience. But at least they lived to look back. Many didn't. This story tells of shocking events that took place in west London during the era of those *"Swinging Sixties."* These events led to the greatest manhunt in British history to trap the killer of a number of prostitutes around the west London district of Hammersmith. The case is one of the last remaining unsolved mass murder sprees in UK crime history. Crimes that shocked and perplexed five decades. This investigation takes a murderous journey through Wales, Scotland and England, touching the world of politics, sport, gangsters and UK celebrities. This book is meant to be informative - not to horrify or entertain.

Hammersmith Broadway early 1960s. Photograph courtesy of Hammersmith and Fulham Archives and Local History Centre. The only part of this scene that is now recognisable is St Paul's Church, Queen Caroline Street.

It is designed, not to disparage the character of these unfortunate women but to help identify the culprit(s) and bring closure for the many surviving family members of these victims. The killer, dubbed *"Jack the Stripper"* or *"The Hammersmith Nudes' Murderer"* was never brought to justice.

The 1969 crime novel *"Goodbye Piccadilly, Farewell Leicester Square"* by Arthur La Bern was loosely based on the Stripper case with the villain strangling women with his necktie. In 1972 it was turned into the movie, *"Frenzy"* by Alfred Hitchcock, with actor Jon Finch playing the protagonist.

Sir Alfred Joseph Hitchcock KBE, 1899-1980 poses (right) with a mock-up newspaper stand during the filming of Frenzy. The cost of reproducing this Getty Image photograph sponsored by Chat magazine.

Chapter 1

The Beginning of Decadence

The 1960s saw a seismic shift in attitudes towards sex and sexuality. Prior to this time, the majority at least showed an air of respectability. But now anything went. The contraceptive pill made casual sex safer and easier – in theory. Abortion and divorce were made easier leading to the so-called *"permissive society."* But this change in attitude towards sex did not mean liberation for women. For some it meant entrapment in a life of vice, violent beatings by pimps and punters alike and sexually transmitted diseases. For some their lives were cruelly cut short. One such victim was twenty-two-year-old Welsh girl Gwynneth Rees.

Gwynneth Rees 1941-1963. The cost of reproducing this Mirrorpix photograph sponsored by Don and Pat Medcalf, Tilleri Gardens, Cwmtillery.

Gwynneth, aged fifteen (in 1957) is the bridesmaid circled. Photograph courtesy of Kim Rees, daughter of Gwynneth.

Gwynneth the third of six children was born on 6th August 1941 in Barry, south Wales. Her parents Gwilym David Henry Rees and Amelia Doreen, née James of 29 Quarella Street, Barry, were initially overjoyed with their tiny bundle of cuddles.

Gwynneth's early life however, was fraught with difficulties, although to outsiders she seemed content. Family members knew that Gwynneth and her father were always at loggerheads and it was only the love shown by her mother that brought her comfort. After leaving Holton Road School, Barry, Gwynneth, five feet two inches in height and brunette took on a number of local factory jobs, one being at the Raygloves glove factory in Barry. She also worked at the Sidroy Mills lingerie factory at Palmerston, Barry, that was opened in 1946 by Jack Feltz, a relative of television and radio personality Vanessa Feltz. In June 1957 Gwynneth attended the wedding of her twenty-two-year-old brother and his nineteen-year-old fiancée (names will be withheld).

Gwynneth's life was completely turned upside down shortly afterwards when Amelia died in the autumn of 1957. She was just forty-six years of age. Gwynneth became totally dissatisfied with her home life and ran away on a number of occasions.

In the summer of 1958 she left home at Lower Gladstone Road, Barry, for good. On the morning that she left she was seen by a number of workmates who were on their way to work at Sidroy Mills. She told her friends, including overlocker Irene Dimond, whom she used to sit next to at the factory, that she was off to London. She disappeared into the distance clutching her worldly possessions in a brown paper bag. On and off she stayed with her married sister, June Oakley (pseudonym) at 3 Letzen Road, Canvey Island in Essex. At the age of seventeen she discovered that she was pregnant and in August 1958 while living at 3 Letzen Road, gave birth to a daughter Kim and registered the birth at Thurrock in Essex. June looked after Kim while Gwynneth went out to work at the Thomas Bata shoe factory at East Tilbury. June eventually brought Kim up as her own child and Gwynneth found herself seeking her pot of gold in London. Instead she found pots of trouble. (O how the gold that shines becomes dim... Lamentations 4v1.) Using the alias Tina Smart she ended up in a life of vice and destitution.

She had many convictions for soliciting and the only time she had a break from the profession was when she was imprisoned on numerous occasions. In London on 27th December 1962 Gwynneth gave birth again, this time to a son, Peter. She took him to Canvey Island where her sister arranged for a local woman to care for him and she went back to London. Peter's birth wasn't legally registered.

Gwynneth, who for most of her short adult life was looked upon by many as garbage, ended up as such. On Friday 8th November 1963 at Richmond and Barnes Councils' refuse tip near the River Thames at Mortlake in London, her badly decomposed body was found amongst waste matter by a council digger driver.

The Refuse Transfer Station after the discovery of Rees' body and as it is today.

The driver, Patrick Cyril Dineen aged twenty-three of 20 Sinclair Road, Kensington (now Hammersmith), uncovered the body while loading a lorry with clinker from the old Destructor Works. The lorry driver Peter Taffurelli had been contracted to haul the clinker that was to be used in road construction. The site was formerly used as a waste incinerator but at the time of the discovery of the body, it was used as a rubbish dump.

Clue of the tattered nylon

Daily Mirror

3d.   Saturday, November 9, 1963   ◆   No. 18,628

GIRL DEAD IN PIT—MURDER PROBE STARTS

Now for the big Commons battle..

By WILLIAM GREIG

THE trial of strength between Prime Minister Sir Alec Douglas-Home and Labour leader Harold Wilson begins next Tuesday when Parliament meets again.

The fireworks should not be long delayed, for with the approach of a General Election, both parties are keyed up—and their leaders will respond to this mood. Labour will get the first big cheer of the session when the winner of the Luton by-election, Mr. Will Howie, takes his seat.

First

He will take precedence over Sir Alec—yesterday's victor in the Kinross by-election — because the Luton result was declared first.

After the new M.P.s have taken their seats, first business will be the Queen's Speech, setting out the Government's programme from now until the General Election.

● Lord Hailsham, who is to renounce his peerage, was selected last night as prospective Parliamentary candidate for St. Marylebone. The present M.P., Sir Wavell Wakefield, is to become a peer.

5r Alec the winner —See Page Two.

IT'S RAIN IN SPAIN FOR ALEX

PRINCESS Alexandra and her husband, Mr. Angus Ogilvy, flew into Madrid last night—in a rainstorm.

This picture shows them just before they boarded

their plane at London Airport yesterday.

The 26-year-old Princess, who is expecting a baby in the New Year, wore an eye-catching fluffy hat and a full coat.

It was a trip Mr. Ogilvy, who is going to see a business friend in Madrid, planned to make alone.

But then, five days ago, a thief broke into the couple's new home in Richmond

Park, Surrey, and stole jewellery—now thought to be worth more than the £5,040 originally estimated.

And Princess Alexandra decided that she did not want to stay behind there without her husband.

By MIRROR REPORTERS

A LONG-HIDDEN murder was revealed yesterday when the naked, headless body of a girl was found in a rubbish dump.

And last night Scotland Yard's top detectives were tackling one of their most gruesome puzzles.

Their only clue was a tattered nylon stocking found on the left leg of the girl—a brunette in her twenties.

A mechanical shovel lifting loads of ash, to be used in road work, unearthed the body from a pit a few feet away from the Thames towpath at Mortlake, between Chiswick and Kew bridges.

Council workman Patrick Dinnen, 23, of Sinclair-road, Kensington, who was operating the mechanical shovel, saw legs dangling from the ash he was lifting.

Then, a few feet away in the dump, he saw a head.

Murder Squad detectives under Chief Superintendent Jack Mannings, went to the dump.

Last night, a police guard was put on the dump, and today they will sift through hundreds of tons of ash for the murder weapon and other possible clues.

Couples

Mr. Frank Bennett, 54-year-old night watchman at the Barnes Corporation destructor in Townsend-road, Mortlake, said last night:

"This road leading to the dump is a favourite haunt for courting couples."

The dead girl had lain underneath 2ft. of tightly-packed ash at the dump — owned by Barnes Council — for several months, detectives thought.

Police said last night that it was still too early to discover how the girl died.

The body was taken to Kingston Hospital, where a post-mortem examination will be performed today.

Baby is stabbed to death

By MIRROR REPORTER

A HUNDRED detectives were knocking on doors early today, after a baby girl was found murdered.

Three-year-old Paula Atkinson was found by two youths.

She had been stabbed. Her body lay in long grass in Jackson's Field, a quarter of a mile from her home in Parbrook-close, Huyton, Liverpool.

Twopence

Last night a neighbour, 15-year-old Marie Murphy, said: "I saw Paula and her sister Marie, who is seven, in a shop in Hillside-avenue, not far away from here.

"Paula had twopence in

Continued on Back Page

Scobie's in front

But look out

here's Lester

IT'S the last lap in the struggle for the 1963 jockeys' championship.

The reigning champion, Scobie Breasley, has ridden 176 winners; Lester Piggott, the challenger, has ridden 174.

They clash for the last time this season at Manchester today. And last night bookmakers were offering 3—1 against Piggott winning the championship outright, and 7-2 against a dead-heat.

No bets were being taken on Breasley.

Both jockeys have four rides each today.

Newsboy's big race nap—See Page 26.

IN THE MIRROR NEXT WEEK.. **DONALD ZEC picks three GREAT girls**

Front page of the Daily Mirror on 9th November 1963. © Mirrorpix.

The police were called to the dump at Townmead Road, which was situated at the rear of the Thames towpath and adjacent to Hammersmith (New) Cemetery. They quickly cordoned off the area and pursued investigations.

Frank Bennett aged fifty-four the night watchman at the site, told the police that the road leading to the small site where the dump was located was a favourite haunt for courting couples. (It seems odd that a person could dig a makeshift grave at the site without being concerned that it was being guarded. It is very unlikely that the body would have been buried during the day with people continually visiting the openly exposed amenity site with their rubbish.)

Detective Superintendent Jack Mannings.
In September 1956, DS Mannings led the Scotland Yard inquiry into the death of Cardiff newly-wed Jean Chalinder née Wilson aged thirty-three. She had been found murdered in a wooded area known as The Plantation at Llanederyn near Cardiff. This still unsolved murder in turn was later linked to another still unsolved murder in Cranford Woods near Heathrow Airport. Mother of two Muriel Maitland was found suffocated and strangled on 30th April 1957. The cost of reproducing this Metropolitan Police Authority image sponsored by Jason and Phillippa Mainwaring, Cwmtillery.

It was ascertained that the body, which had been badly damaged by the action of the digger driver, was naked but for one nylon stocking rolled down to the ankle of the left leg. A number of teeth were missing which didn't become significant until some time later. The police, under Detective Superintendent Frederick Chadburn and Detective Superintendent Jack Mannings, had the mammoth task of finding out who the victim was and more importantly how she had died.

A police guard was stationed at the dump and the following day hundreds of tons of ash were sifted in the hope of finding a possible murder weapon or other clues. The victim had been buried two feet deep in the tightly compacted ash. Five days after the discovery, the police started preparing a questionnaire for residents, riverside boating clubs and businesses based near the rubbish tip.

One theory the police had was that the victim may have been accosted and murdered as she lay sunbathing on the Thames towpath.

The body was first taken to Kingston Hospital for a post-mortem examination and was then taken to Guy's Hospital, Southwark, for medical and scientific experts to piece together the victim's appearance. The method used to accomplish this was based on the forensic technique employed to solve the murders of two unidentified women in Scotland in 1935. Their dismembered bodies were found wrapped in newspapers and dumped in a stream near Moffat in Dumfriesshire. There, scientists used fledgling forensic anthropology to superimpose a photograph of one of the suspected victims Isabella Kerr, over the X-ray of her skull. By the time the experts had finished, a picture was built up that led to the two women being formally identified. They were Isabella Kerr and her housekeeper Mary Jane Rogerson. Kerr was the common-law wife of Bombay born Dr Bukhtyar Rustomji Ratanji Hakim of Lancaster, England. The doctor, who had changed his name by deed poll to Buck Ruxton, was arrested and charged with the murder of both women. At his eleven-day trial that ended on 13th March 1936, he was found guilty on two counts of murder. He was hanged at Strangeways Prison, Manchester on 12th May 1936. He was thirty-six years of age.

Dr Buck Ruxton 1899-1936. Ruxton thought he had committed the perfect murder. After killing his common-law wife and his housekeeper he cut up and mutilated their bodies beyond recognition.
He then parcelled up the pieces in old newspapers and took them one hundred miles away and dumped them in a stream, believing there was nothing that could lead the police back to him. Unfortunately for him the papers were Lancaster editions and the paper trail did lead back to him. He may as well have labelled the parcels: 'If undelivered please return to Buck Ruxton.'

An examination by pathologist Professor Arthur Keith Mant soon revealed that the Mortlake victim, who had been deliberately buried under several feet of clinker, might have been dead for several months. Professor Mant and his team worked feverishly to reconstruct the skull of the deceased and gradually built up a *"portrait"* of the dead woman. She had five teeth missing from her upper jaw and three from her lower.

Professor Arthur Keith Mant MRCS (Eng) LRCP (Lond) MB BS (Lond) MD (Lond) FRCPath FRCP (Lond) DMJ (Path) 11th September 1919 – 11th October 2000. His father was George Mant, a solicitor who represented the tenth generation of members of the legal profession in the family. Professor Mant chose not to follow in his father's footsteps and in 1939 enrolled in an Undergraduate Course at St Mary's Medical School London. He became a British forensic pathologist who headed the Special Medical Section of the British Army's War Crimes Group, which investigated Nazi war crimes committed during World War II.
Photograph of Professor Mant in his office at Guy's Hospital Medical School in 1981 courtesy of Professor Stephen Cordner, Victorian Institute of Forensic Medicine, Victoria, Australia, and by kind permission of Professor Mant's son Professor Timothy GK Mant.

A spokesman for the murder squad told the press: *'It is a question now of waiting for the findings of the scientists. We have had enquiries from many people who think the girl may fit the description of either a daughter or a relative, and we are making a careful examination of them all.'*

Two weeks after the discovery of the body the following appeal was issued from the *"murder room"* at Richmond police station:-

'On 8th November the body of an unknown woman was found buried on a rubbish dump owned by Barnes Council at Townmead Road, which is adjacent to the towpath of the River Thames. Police at Richmond police station appeal to all landladies, parents, guardians and employers who may have knowledge of a missing woman between the age group of eighteen to twenty-seven years, height 5ft 1in to 5ft 5ins, long face, well nourished, to come forward and assist them in establishing the identity of this person. Please communicate with Richmond 1113 or any police station.'

The digger that unearthed the body of Gwynneth Rees. A detective examines the legs that are hanging from the bucket.

An important breakthrough for the police came when Gwynneth's married sister June Oakley from Canvey Island reported her concerns to the police that Gwynneth had seemingly disappeared without trace. She said that Gwynneth had been expected as a guest at the wedding of their sister Margaret who had married her fiancé Glynn Davies at Dinas Powis, East Glamorgan, on 19th October 1963. June said that there was something dreadfully amiss as she had been unable to contact Gwynneth for weeks prior to the wedding. Armed with this information and from fingerprints taken from the body, the identity of the deceased soon became apparent.

When the body which had been discovered at Mortlake had been formally identified, a journalist from the *'Barry and District News and Barry Herald'* interviewed Gwynneth's married brother, twenty-eight-year-old David a process worker of 45 Laura Street, Barry.

Speaking of the time when Gwynneth had left home, he said: *'She was then sixteen, very lively and independent…. It was in the following year that she came back to see [our] father, but stayed only a day or so. I saw her for only twenty minutes and she said very little….'* On Tuesday 26th November, eighteen days after the discovery of the body, eight men were questioned at Richmond police station about Gwynneth's acquaintances and movements, although they were released shortly afterwards without charge. Members of the murder squad scoured East End pubs and cafés interviewing scores of men and women. They learned that Gwynneth Rees was also known as Georgette Rees, Tina Smart and Tina Dawson. She had lived in Stepney, east London, from 1959 until the 7th August 1963. It was ascertained that she had lived in a basement flat at 27 Warriner Gardens, Battersea, from 8th August to 12th September 1963 and then at 4 Hague Street Buildings, Bethnal Green, until her disappearance.

It now looked likely that she had been dead for no more than six weeks when her body had been discovered at Mortlake.

According to David Seabrook in his 2006 book *"Jack of Jumps"* published by Granta Books London, the infamous gangland twins Reginald and Ronald Kray were both interviewed about the murder of Gwynneth. On 27th January 1964 a meeting between the police and the Krays took place in the office of their solicitor, Mr Sampson.

He had already advised the twins not to answer any questions about the matter and they duly obeyed. When invited by the police to look at a photograph of Gwynneth Rees, Reginald Kray refused. It is not known for sure whether the Krays actually knew Gwynneth although it was quite likely owing to their involvement in the vice business. What is known for certain is that Cornelius Whitehead, an associate of the twins had known her. He had *"ponced"* on her for several months leading up to April 1963.

In March 1969 at the Old Bailey, Cornelius Whitehead was sentenced to seven years imprisonment for accessory to the murder of Jack *"The Hat"* McVitie at Evering Road, Stoke Newington in October 1967. McVitie had been lured to a party by the Kray twins, and was stabbed to death by Reginald Kray.

Justice also caught up with the identical twins when they were both given identical sentences of life imprisonment for their part in the murder of McVitie and of rival gang member George Cornell who had been shot dead by Ronald Kray on 9th March 1966.

On Wednesday 13th November 1963, at Kingston Coroner's Court the deputy coroner Dr William Reginald Huleatt Heddy opened the inquest into the death of Gwynneth Rees. Formal evidence of the discovery of the body was given and the digger driver Patrick Dineen gave Dr Heddy the following evidence: *'I was clearing some rubbish and loading clinker when the shovel picked up what at first I thought was the body of an animal and I noticed a very strong smell. I put the shovel into the heap again and saw two legs hanging from the shovel. I stopped the machine and shouted to the foreman [Edward Kimpton of 85 Chertsey Court, Lower Richmond Road, Mortlake] that I believed I had uncovered a body. Later the police arrived. At the time of the discovery of the body I was working about twenty-five yards from the Thames towpath. There was no fence or wall dividing the towpath from the dump.'*

Dr Heddy then asked Detective Sergeant Minors questions about the state of the recovered body, finishing with: *"I understand the head was detached from the body?"* DS Minors replied: *"Yes sir."* The hearing was then adjourned until 11th December when it was further adjourned until 4th March 1964. This was to give the police more time to continue their inquiries. (Up until the 22nd November 1963, the suspicious death of Gwynneth Rees was splashed all over the London and Welsh newspapers. However on that date and for a long period thereafter, the assassination of American president John F Kennedy stole the headlines pushing Rees' death into the background.)

The resumed inquest was heard on 4th March 1964 at Kingston Coroner's Court before the coroner Dr Cyril Faudel Joseph Baron and jury. Pathologist, Professor Arthur Keith Mant told the inquest that it was impossible to say for certain the cause of death owing to the decomposition of the body. He said that there were no fractures of the skeleton but that did not preclude the possibility of violence prior to death. He said that in his opinion, Rees was most probably strangled and her clothing taken off her after she had died.

Detective Chief Inspector Peter Vibart said that the police had interviewed 1,135 persons in connection with Rees' death but could find no one that had seen her after the end of September 1963. He said that she had eleven convictions for prostitution and one for larceny, all in the East End of London.

Mrs Brenda Margaret Meah, of Grosvenor Buildings, Poplar, said that she had known the deceased and that she was a prostitute. She said that she last saw her in a café in Cannon Street Road, Stepney, one Saturday in September 1963, but could not say for certain which one. As they were talking Rees confided that she was pregnant and planned to self-abort.

Brenda said: *'I told her not to be silly. I invited her to come to my house the following day for dinner but she failed to turn up.'* The coroner asked: *'Do you know anyone who ill-treated Rees?'* to which she replied: *'Yes. She was given a good hiding one day. I told the police all about it.'*

Victor Martin Hatt of Belton Way, Bow, told the inquest that he had lived with Rees at 4 Hague Street Buildings, Bethnal Green. He admitted knowing that she was a prostitute and candidly admitted that he had lived off her immoral earnings. He said the last time he saw her was on 28th September 1963. He said that he was aware that someone had given her a good beating some time before she vanished but didn't know that she had been pregnant and didn't know anything about how she had died.

Sydney Herbert Saunders, the landlord of the Hague Street property where Rees had lived, told the inquest that he last saw her on 27th September1963. She had told him that she was pregnant and that she was going to get some pills to get rid of the baby. He too had been aware that Rees had been given a good hiding by someone and he had informed the police about this. (It turned out that the alleged *"giver of the good hiding"* was the Kray twins' accomplice Cornelius Whitehead.) Asked by the coroner if he had any idea how Rees had got to the refuse tip at Mortlake, he replied: *'The only thing I can think of was she had been picked up by clients.'*

Summing up, Dr Baron told the jury: *'One can conjecture, one can wonder, was she perhaps murdered, or did she or somebody else attempt to abort her pregnancy of which we have been told. These are questions that cannot be answered.'*

Following an adjournment to consider the case the jury returned an *'open verdict.'*

Gwynneth Rees was buried at St Katherine's Church, Canvey Island, Essex on 11th March 1964. If Gwynneth's father Gwilym had grieved over her death, his grief would have been temporary. He himself died of cancer just a few months later in Barry.

Gwynneth's sister June and five-year-old Kim left Canvey Island six weeks after the funeral and moved back to Wales. Kim, who for many years believed that Gwynneth had been her aunt, had a nervous breakdown when she found out the truth.

The aluminium cross was erected by Gwynneth's brother-in-law. The flower vase nearest the cross is inscribed: Gwyn. Dear Auntie of Gary, Kim and Lynn. The other vase is inscribed: From Brenda and ???? The name of the second person has been deliberately defaced. Brenda Meah and another unknown person were the only friends of Gwynneth who attended her funeral. Kim was later to learn that she was actually the daughter of Gwynneth not a niece.

Now recovered and accepting the situation, Kim appreciates that although her mother had led an unsavoury life, if it hadn't been for her, she her five children and her four grandchildren wouldn't be alive today. Kim was diagnosed with multiple myeloma (cancer of the bone marrow) in November 2000.

Kim is here pictured chatting to Prince Charles at the opening day of the new George Thomas Hospice, Whitchurch, Cardiff on 14th July 2005. Photograph courtesy of Kim Rees.

She is currently receiving treatment at Llandough Hospital, Penarth. Her condition is incurable but thankfully, remissions have been induced with treatment. Kim's brother Peter, who had been given a new identity after his birth, left Canvey Island in 2007 to live in Spain. It is not known if he knows the truth about his mother or that he has a sister living in Wales.

Robert Hale (pseudonym) from Canvey Island knew Gwynneth Rees well. He had been in Gwynneth's house at 3 Letzen Road, when she started complaining of having labour pains with Kim. Robert, then aged fourteen, ran to his mother's house nearby to summon help. He remembers one night a few years later in the 1960s, when a number of cars pulled up outside the front of the house where Gwynneth was living. All the cars had their headlights on full beam and it resembled a scene from a gangster movie.

The occupants of the cars had come to intimidate Gwynneth. It is believed that the gang had travelled from London to Canvey Island to put pressure on Gwynneth for leaving her pimp. This account is backed up by Gwynneth's daughter Kim who had the same story related to her by her aunt who was an eyewitness to the event. The last time Robert Hale saw Gwynneth was in the West End of London shortly before her death. He said: *'As I was walking towards her I could see she was with two men, one either side of her, and she appeared to be being led where she didn't want to go. As I was getting nearer to her and about to talk to her she looked at me intently and shook her head as if to say: "Don't get involved." 'I never saw Gwynneth again.'* (One of the two men died in March 2010.)

Chapter 2

Suspicious Death at Hammersmith

The jury reached their verdict into the death of Gwynneth Rees on 4th March 1964, with the knowledge that one month earlier, on Sunday 2nd February, the body of another prostitute, thirty-year-old Hannah Tailford was found on the foreshore of the Thames near Hammersmith Bridge, less than two miles from where Gwynneth's body had been found.

She had left home, Top Flat, 37 Thurlby Road, West Norwood, London, on Friday 24th January 1964. Nine days later her body was found naked except for her nylon stockings rolled down to the ankles and her semen stained panties stuffed into her mouth. The earlier verdict into the death of Gwynneth Rees had puzzled many and led to speculation. Was she murdered? What self-respecting prostitute would ply her trade on a stinking rubbish tip wearing just one stocking? She had no reason to be there.

Was there a connection between her death and the death of Hannah Tailford? One puzzling feature for the Gwynneth Rees murder inquiry team was: *Just what had Gwynneth, who had been living in Bethnal Green, east London been doing in the Hammersmith district of west London?*' Likewise, a puzzling feature for the Hannah Tailford murder inquiry team was: *'What had Tailford, from West Norwood, been doing in Hammersmith?'* Tailford's body had been found under a floating pontoon at the London Corinthian Sailing Club, Upper Mall, Hammersmith. The finder was Douglas Timothy Capon, aged twenty-three, a truck driver who lived at 59 Yeldham Road, Hammersmith. Douglas and his brother, twenty-year-old shipping clerk George Monty Capon, were members of the London Corinthian Sailing Club; at that time the Thames top dinghy-racing club. The brothers had been bailing water out of a rescue launch at the sailing club at 1.15pm, when Douglas noticed the body that had been partly hidden by driftwood, and a discarded Christmas tree. Douglas stood guard over the body while George contacted the police at Linden House, the headquarters of the sailing club. Tailford's body had been lying on its right side facing the river with the feet pointing towards Hammersmith Bridge.

Inspector James Robert Meyler and PCs Roger Clarke, Royston Rees, Brian Hourne and PC Furey attended the scene within fifteen minutes of the discovery of the body. PC Royston Rees quickly left the scene, returned to Hammersmith police station and telephoned the Divisional Surgeon, Dr Joshua Stein of 231 King Street Hammersmith.

Rees returned to the murder scene and Dr Stein arrived shortly afterwards and pronounced life extinct. At 3.30pm staff from the funeral firm of Arthur Luckett of 35 Glenthorne Road, Hammersmith, arrived at the scene to remove the body to Hammersmith

Mortuary. (Arthur's unofficial slogan was: "If you kicked the bucket come to Arthur Luckett.")

Detective Inspector Reuben Ridge (third from right) with other police officers at the murder scene. Hammersmith Bridge can be seen in the background. The cost of reproducing this Getty Image photograph sponsored by Chat magazine.

The police were certain that the victim was still alive when she was dumped in the Thames and had then floated under the wooden pier that was chained to the river wall. The day after the discovery, pathologist Dr Donald Teare carried out an examination of the body at Hammersmith Mortuary. He noted that the deceased was: *'Sparely built but adequately nourished adult woman 5 ft 2 ins in height. A pair of knickers was stuffed into the mouth. There was an old surgical scar on the lower abdomen and gross linear striae were seen on the abdomen. The hair was dark brown, and the eyes were brown…. The fingernails were bitten down to the quick. The skin was waterlogged and the body covered with mud… There was a post-mortem wound…on the back of the right calf…'* Dr Teare concluded that the victim had died from drowning.

Detective Chief Superintendent Benjamin Devonald of Scotland Yard, fronted the Tailford murder inquiry aided by Detective Chief Superintendent Frederick Chadburn and Detective Inspector Reuben Ridge, a former Flying Squad Officer, but who had by then attained the position as Head of Thames Division CID. Also closely involved in the inquiry was Detective Sergeant James Patrick Emons. By studying the tides and the currents of the Thames, the police tried to work out the area in which Tailford most likely entered or was put into the water. They deduced the most likely places would have been Chelsea or Fulham. They believed that they were on the verge of identifying the body when John Halpin contacted the police the day after its discovery. He said that his Glasgow-born wife Jane aged twenty-four had not returned to their home at Roman Road, East Ham, after leaving three weeks earlier. He was taken to the mortuary but was relieved to find that the body was not that of his wife.

Dr Robert Donald Teare. MA, MD, FRCP, FRCPath LLD, DMJ. 1911-1979. He was President of the Medico-Legal Society 1965-1967. Dr Teare was also involved in the post-mortems of The Beatles' manager Brian Epstein in 1967 and rocker Jimi Hendrix in 1970. Photograph courtesy of Gillian Kirk.

Detective Chief Superintendent Benjamin Devonald, 1915-1965. Artwork provided by Tomas Jones, Brynmawr Foundation School. © 2011, Tomas Jones. The cost of reproducing this artwork sponsored by Jane Wilson, Abertillery.

The body at Hammersmith Mortuary was initially identified from fingerprints taken. They corresponded with prints on police file and revealed that the victim was indeed thirty-year-old Hannah Tailford. Her sister Mrs Elsie Youngman of 99 North Road, Ponteland, Newcastle-upon-Tyne formally identified the body on 5th February at the Mortuary.

Hannah Tailford was born at Bluebell Cottages, Heddon-on-the-Wall, Northumberland, on 19th August 1933 to John and Elsie Tailford. At the time of her birth her ten-year-old sister Elsie excitedly greeted her into the world. The tears of joy however soon turned to tears of despair. By 1949 Tailford had been sent to an approved school for stealing as it was recognised that she needed care and attention. At that age (sixteen) she was already staying out all night and going with men. After three years in an approved school in Liverpool she returned home for six months but then just walked out. Within one week she was picked up by the police in London and returned to the approved school.

After six months she again returned home but vanished shortly afterwards and was arrested at the docks in South Shields. By this time Tailford's mother was on the verge of a nervous breakdown and the family refused to have her back home. She was placed in a hostel but after absconding she was sent to Borstal.

John and Elsie Tailford. Photograph courtesy of Hannah Tailford's son Stephen Sloman.

Hannah Tailford on the right in the late 1940s. Photograph courtesy of Hannah's son Stephen Sloman.

With all that behind her, she then lived in many areas of London and worked as a machinist, a domestic and as a waitress. She had used many aliases including Anne Taylor, Anne Lynch, Hannah Lynch and Theresa Bell. The inquest into the death of Hannah Tailford was opened at Hammersmith Coroner's Court by coroner Dr Gavin Thurston on Wednesday 5th February 1964 and was adjourned until Wednesday 8th April when a further adjournment was granted until Tuesday 28th April.

The resumed inquest heard before a jury on 28th April revealed some shocking facts. Detective Chief Superintendent Benjamin Devonald told the court: *'Miss Tailford was a "sexual pervert." She was known to have attended parties at which sexual orgies took place. There is also evidence that she was in the habit of taking 'purple heart' tablets. Miss Tailford has been convicted for prostitution three times, the last occasion being in January 1963. She used to frequent cafés and coffee stalls in the Charing Cross, Victoria,*

Shepherds Bush and Finsbury Park areas. She would go with clients and she was prone to discard her clothing.'

PAGE 2 DAILY MIRROR, Wednesday, February 5, 1964.

RIVER NUDE: MAN HELPS YARD

A MAN was helping police with their inquiries into the dead nude riddle early today.

The man—a billiards hall manager who knew the dead woman well—walked into Lavender Hill police station,

Wandsworth, late last night.

Later he was taken to Hammersmith, where he was interviewed by Murder Squad detectives.

The dead woman, whose naked body was found in the Thames at the weekend, was named yesterday as good-time girl Hannah Tailford, 31.

She came to London

about five years ago from Heddon-on-the-Wall, Northumberland.

Last night detectives were searching for her daughter, a three-year-old named Linda. The dead woman also had an 18-month-old son.

The detectives know that the little girl has been looked after by friends.

Appeal

And they believe that if they find Linda, it may help them to trace her mother's killer.

Last night Scotland Yard issued a picture and appealed for information from anyone who knew her.

Detectives know she had used several other names—including Anne Tailford, Teresa Bell and Anne Taylor—and that she had many men friends.

Hannah Tailford . . . she used several names

Caught—after 111 days

THE "Tattooed Man" was back in jail last night—after 111 days on the run from Dartmoor.

Tattooed Jack Marsh, 41, vanished from a quarry working-party outside Dartmoor last October.

He dodged the police until Monday, when he was spotted by two detec-

tives making routine inquiries in a street in Caterham, Surrey.

When he escaped, Marsh, of Shakespeare - avenue, Ipswich, had served two months of a five-year sentence for receiving and for assaulting a policeman.

It was his third jailbreak since 1950.

BBC BRING BACK TV FOR WIVES

THE BBC is to bring back T V programmes for women, following protests against the scrapping of the programmes last year.

A new-style regular magazine series is to be launched, specially aimed at women viewers.

Final details have yet to be worked out.

Family

But it is known that the new programmes will also contain family items of interest to husbands and children as well as wives.

Doreen Stephens, who ran the BBC TV women's programmes for ten years until they were dropped, will be in charge of the new venture.

I T V does not run special programmes for women.'

Sailor William ha with women—40

MERCHANT Navy officer William Parry had a way with the women. He had affairs with forty of them.

The secret of his romantic past came out in the Divorce Court yesterday when he sought a decree against his wife, Glen.

Listed

Judge Wingate-Saul was handed a document in which Mr. Parry listed the women with whom he had had affairs during the 9½ years of his marriage.

"That is as many as I have seen in a discretion statement," he said.

But he granted a decree

POSTMEN KNOCK FOR MPs

By MIRROR REPORTER

FOUR HUNDRED indignant postmen "knocked" at Parliament's door yesterday.

They went to the Commons to protest to their local M Ps against the proposed unaddressed circulars delivery service.

The men object to the G P O plan because, they say, it will interfere with the quality of the postal service.

Meantime, in the debating chamber, Postmaster-General Reginald Bevins was talking about "the friendly postman."

Refused

He refused, however, to abandon the new service.

Mr. Bevins was speaking in the "mailbag storm" debate.

This arose because the right-wing Aims of Industry organisation plan to use the service to deliver anti-nationalisation leaflets.

And Labour put down a motion condemning the use of a public service for the distribution of political propaganda.

Leading the attack, the Party's deputy leader Mr. George Brown said that householders might find some circulars offensive.

The Labour motion was defeated by 73 votes.

FORCES' PAY RISE OUT TOMORROW

Higher pay scales for the Forces are to be announced by the Government tomorrow.

It is expected that the new scales will give an increase of about 1s. in the £, as exclusively forecast in the Daily Mirror.

IT'S BOOM-TIME FOR BRITAIN

By ROBERT HEAD

BRITAIN'S economic outlook won three massive votes of confidence yesterday. There was CONFIDENCE from the foreigners who are backing Britain with cash and export orders.

This shows up in our gold and foreign currency reserves, which jumped another £6,000,000 to £953,000,000 last month the Treasury revealed.

Reserves have now been rising for ten months running. It is a sign that overseas investors are content to leave money in London without fear that a trade crisis will threaten the £.

CONFIDENCE from wage-earners, who borrowed another £7,000,000 on hire-purchase in December, pushing the nation's "Never-Never" debt up to £954,000,000, the highest for more than two years.

Today's weather

Sunny spells, showers. Cold. OUTLOOK: Similar.

London area, E. Anglia, Midlands, E. England: Sunny periods, and showers, night frost. Max. temp. 5 C (41 F).

S.E. and Central-S. England: Sunny periods, isolated showers in north. Max. temp 6 C (43 F).

Channel Islands, S.W. England, S. Wales and Mon.: Sunny periods. Max. temp. 7 C (45 F).

DAILY MIRRO

THE GIR THE MO

WHAT a real pl Russia's Valen the first woman in guest in this countr

London Airport to be monopolised flying to or from cr

It makes a splen welcome a famous y whose Space feat l the whole world—r national or politica

Mara

Remember that a Adam-and-Eve Spa when Valentina and (male) were orbitin at the same time, a of each other at mo

Remember how V off in her Space shi apologised for falli Remember how she she flashed through she reported to Eart pencil she used for t had broken !

Later, at Moscow's year, golden-haired V another cosmonaut. Russia's most celebra

Deligl

No doubt about it young career girl is with the mostest. First Space bride, the first cosmonaut and the Queen will to talk to each othe Palace today.

Proud to have you

Page two of the Daily Mirror on Wednesday 5th February 1964. © Mirrorpix.

Despite earlier assumptions, Devonald said that the most likely place where Miss

Tailford's body had entered the Thames was at Duke's Meadow, Chiswick, which was frequented by a large number of prostitutes. It was easy for a motorist to drive up in a vehicle and dump a body into the river.

Devonald concluded his evidence by stating that during the previous three months over 700 persons had been interviewed in connection with the case. Tailford's sister, Elsie Youngman told the inquest: '*I last saw my sister alive in Newcastle in 1960. She was with a "Jock Lynch" who I had believed was her husband. I first met Lynch on the Whitsun weekend in 1958 when Hannah had brought him to visit our mother. They visited mother again in October 1958, stayed a month and then they moved into rooms in the Jesmond area of Newcastle. They returned to London in January or February 1959. I did not hear from her again until eighteen months ago [actually twenty two months ago] when she was in hospital to say she had had a baby boy the previous day. [Lawrence, who was born on 14th May 1962 at St George's Hospital Westminster.] She also said that she had a baby girl called Linda aged thirteen months [born on 7th April 1961 at St George's Hospital Westminster]. I have not heard anything from her since.*'

Mr Thomas Jones, principal scientific officer at New Scotland Yard told the inquest that a post-mortem examination had shown that Tailford had eaten a meal of bacon, eggs, and cheese shortly before she had entered the water. There was nothing to suggest that she had consumed alcohol or drugs.

Mr Allan Lynch aged thirty-one told the inquest that his real name was William Ewing and that he had been born on 2nd June 1932 at Scranton, Pennsylvania, USA. He said he first met Hannah in 1955 and that they had lived together from 1956 until the day she had disappeared. He said that they had a child named Linda who was born on 6th April 1961. (She was actually born on 7th April.) He said: '*To my knowledge she had three other children, one who she said was a boy and who was born before I knew her. I don't know what became of this child. The second child, also a boy was born in St Stephen's Hospital [Fulham] in about 1959. He was adopted by some people from the Midlands. They took the baby away on the day she left hospital after the birth. The next child was Linda born in 1961. The last child, a boy was born in St George's Hospital [Westminster] about September or October 1962. I never saw this child. When I collected Hannah from the hospital, she told me the child was being kept in. I made no further enquiries.*' (There are glaring differences in the statement Lynch gave to the coroner and the reality of things. He stated that he had lived with Tailford from 1956 until she vanished, yet he failed to mention that on 1st July 1957 in Exeter she had given birth to a son Stephen Michael Tailford, now Stephen Michael Sloman. A possible reason for this omission could have been because he was afraid of implicating himself for abandoning Stephen. He also said that the last child was a boy born in September or October 1962. Lynch could have been mistaken but in reality, the child, Lawrence Tailford was born on 14th May 1962.)

Lynch said that Hannah would go out every evening at around 9.30pm and return around 6.00am the following morning. He also said he had believed she had been employed as a cashier in an all-night restaurant at Southwark Bridge Road. He said the last time he saw her alive was at 9.00pm on Friday 24th January 1964, when she had made a puzzling comment to their three-year-old daughter Linda as she was leaving home. She had said: '*How would you like a new mother?*'

Mr Arnold Henry Downton aged forty-two, a railway shunter of 189 King's Cross Road, Holborn, told the inquest that he had been friendly with Miss Tailford. The only man she ever spoke about was a *"Tony."* Downton said that he and his common-law wife Elizabeth Ritchie-Downton aged twenty-eight met Miss Tailford whom they both knew as *"Doll"* at about 6.30pm on Friday 31st January 1964 at Charing Cross. She had told them that she was starving so they took her to the nearby Florence Café in Villiers Street and bought her a meal and had also given her 5 shillings (twenty-five pence). She had looked miserable and had been crying. She told them that she was fed up and was contemplating ending her life. Downton said he told her not to be so daft.

With the evidence given by Lynch regarding Tailford saying to her daughter, *'How would you like a new mother?'* and Henry Downton's evidence that Tailford had made a comment to him two days before her body was found that she was contemplating suicide, it may have appeared to some at the inquest that a ruling of suicide would be handed down by the jury. But there was more to come.

Westminster coroner, Dr Gavin Leonard Bourdas Thurston CBE, MB BS; FRCP DMJ (Hon Causa) 1911-1980. Dr Thurston, in his career had presided over many high profile inquests including the ones into the deaths of former World Light-Heavyweight boxing champion Freddie Mills in 1965, Wizard of Oz actress Judy Garland in 1969, rocker Jimi Hendrix in 1970 and "The Who" drummer Keith Moon in 1978. In 1975 Dr Thurston had issued an arrest warrant for Lord Lucan after an inquest decided that he had murdered Sandra Rivett the family nanny.

Dr Thurston married Ione Barber in 1935. After Ione died he married Dr Janet Hazel in 1969. Two years after Dr Thurston died, Janet married world-renowned pathologist Professor Cedric Keith Simpson (keeping things in the pathological family). Dr Thurston has a grandson also named Gavin Thurston who is a multi-award winning freelance cameraman-director-producer for BBC, ITV, Discovery, Animal Planet etc. Gavin has filmed extensively with Sir David Attenborough for numerous wildlife programmes. Photograph courtesy of Dr Thurston's son, Dr John Thurston.

Pathologist, Dr Donald Teare, next gave evidence that the body had been in the water between two and seven days. (If Arnold Downton's evidence was correct that he had spoken to Tailford on Friday 31st January, then two days in the water would be more like it.) Dr Teare said that he had found bruising on both sides of Tailford's jaw which could have been caused by a blow from a fist or from a fall. He added that he had heard of a case of a woman who had committed suicide putting something in her mouth to stop herself screaming, but it was most unusual for anyone contemplating suicide to eat a large meal shortly beforehand. (It must also have seemed most unusual for a woman before committing suicide to thrust a pair of semen stained knickers into her mouth!) After dozens of witnesses had given evidence at the inquest the coroner said that suicide could not be ruled out altogether, but, it was *"wildly improbable."* Advising the jury to return an *'open verdict,'* he said that returning such a verdict would allow for police investigations to continue and the possibility of justice being done. An *'open verdict'* was reached which then led to the coroner closing the inquest. Hannah Tailford's body was released and taken to Newcastle by her sister Elsie Youngman. There she was cremated.

On Wednesday 3rd June 2009 the author was visited by one of Hannah Tailford's sons; fifty-one-year-old Stephen Michael Sloman who lives in Portsmouth. He brought with him a large file containing over 200 pages of police reports, coroner's inquest papers, and statements from witnesses who had last seen Hannah Tailford shortly before she disappeared. Film producer and director Jeff Leahy, who had produced a television documentary about Hannah Tailford and which featured Stephen, had presented the file to him. A large amount of information presented in this chapter is based on data contained in that file. Stephen had been registered as being born to Hannah Tailford, a manufacturing tailor's machinist at 30, New North Road, Exeter, Devon on 1st July 1957. This address was a women's prison.

Over the next four years Stephen was fostered by a number of different people. One couple in Kensington, London, used to tie him to a chair to get him used to the two large dogs in the house. Dr Lomax Simpson, a child psychologist who took Stephen under her wing in later years, identified this couple to him. Another couple that Dr Simpson refused to identify put Stephen in a container of very hot water for wetting the bed. He was then returned to a children's home with scarring around the groin area. On 11th January 1962 Stephen then aged four was legally adopted by Dennis Arthur Sloman and his wife Daisy Elizabeth Sloman née Agate of Green Hedges Avenue, East Grinstead, Sussex. Dennis who married Daisy in 1952 died in 2004 aged seventy-four, but Daisy was still alive in 2011.

In December 2006 Stephen contacted the Ipswich police regarding the murders of five prostitutes in the Ipswich district between November and December 2006. He informed the police that he was a son of Hannah Tailford and expressed his concern that the Ipswich killer may have possibly read David Seabrook's 2006 book *"Jack of Jumps,"* which dealt with the unsolved murders of eight prostitutes in west London between 1959 and 1965. Stephen believed that the Ipswich killer could possibly be emulating the London killer.

Stephen Sloman in his Royal Navy uniform. Stephen says he always knew that hostilities were on the horizon when BBC War Correspondent Kate Adie turned up. Stephen looks very much like Hannah's father. (See photograph page 20.)

It appeared that the police took Stephen's concerns seriously, asking him where they could obtain a copy of *"Jack of Jumps."* On Saturday 16th December 2006, Marcus Dunk, a journalist with the *'Daily Express'* did a double page feature entitled, *"Mystery of the Serial Strangler."* Dunk noted that eight prostitutes had been strangled and stripped in London by a killer who was never caught. He also noted the astonishing similarities between the vicious killings of more than forty years ago and the Suffolk murders. There were remarkable similarities between the London murders and the Ipswich ones. All the victims were prostitutes, all were found naked, all were dumped in or around water, and all were strangled. Three days after the story broke, on 19th December, Steve Gerald James Wright aged forty-eight was arrested on suspicion of committing the Ipswich murders and after a trial at Ipswich Crown Court which ended on 21st February 2008, he was found guilty on five counts of murder and jailed for life. That guilty verdict brought closure to the families of the Ipswich victims. Stephen Sloman is still waiting for his.

In March 2008 it was announced that Wright would be lodging an appeal against his conviction. He was reported to have written to the court of appeal: *'All five women were stripped naked of clothing/jewellery/phones/bags and no evidence was found in my house or car.'* In February 2009 it was reported that Wright had dropped his bid to lodge an appeal.

Stephen Sloman met his brother Lawrence for the first time in January 2009. He still yearns to make contact with his sister Linda who was taken to Scotland by their father Allan Lynch after Hannah's murder. Stephen is also anxious to trace his brother David John Lynch who was born in 1959.

Apparently he was sold for £20 to a couple in Staffordshire. Tailford had given birth to David John at St Stephen's Hospital, Fulham, on 22nd May 1959. On 5th June, the day that Hannah Tailford was discharged from hospital, the Staffordshire couple handed over the £20 and Tailford handed over the baby. The authorities were well aware of the situation but turned a blind eye believing that David would be better off in care. His birth was never legally registered.

Stephen Michael Sloman in 2009 described himself and his family:

- A Barnado boy, adopted after a turbulent start with fostering.
- An OK student *"could have done better"* the teachers always said, but I just wanted to be a sailor from the start.
- Left school at fifteen and joined the Royal Navy, served all over the world and saw action in the Cod Wars, Cyprus, The Falklands in 1982, and both Gulf Wars.
- Left the Royal Navy after twenty-seven years and started a new career training the next generation of sailors.
- Currently a Training Designer working on MOD contracts.
- Met wife Tula in 1978. She was also in the Royal Navy. (I told her the night I met her that I would marry her and we did marry three months later.)
- Had one daughter Zoe who is currently serving in the Royal Navy with the Bomb Disposal Team.
- Zoe and her partner Doug have three daughters, Bo aged seven, Abbie, aged five, and Evie aged two.

And that's about it. Life has been good to me, and I love every day.

Stephen's wife Tula and "Mum" Daisy Elizabeth Sloman.

Stephen was due to be interviewed in August 2010 by Martin Brunt, a Sky News reporter. The interview was designed for Stephen to explain how he has coped with the knowledge that his mother was the victim of a serial killer. Shortly before the interview Stephen came into contact with Hannah Tailford's brother who was quite seriously ill. Not wishing to cause any upset to his uncle he declined to be interviewed. His uncle died at the end of August 2010.

Chapter 3

Murder at Chiswick

F ive years prior to Hannah Tailford's demise, the body of a twenty-one-year-old prostitute, Elizabeth Figg, was found at Duke's Meadow Chiswick. She was found on Wednesday 17th June 1959 with several teeth missing. Duke's Meadow was where it was believed Hannah Tailford's body had been deposited in the Thames. Figg had been murdered and her killer was still at large.

Duke's Meadow, Chiswick. Figg was placed in a sitting position against this tree facing the river.
The cost of reproducing this Mirrorpix photograph sponsored by Blaenau Gwent County Borough Council and UK Steel Enterprise Limited.

Figg, who had last been seen in Holland Park in the early hours of 17th June, was found dead just a few hours later in long grass under a willow tree on the Thames river-bank. The area was at the rear of the Ibis sports ground. Described as 5ft 2ins tall, dark hair, slim, with discoloured teeth, her barefooted body wearing a navy-blue and white striped summer dress, was found at 5.15am by PC Mills of Chiswick police.

He had been taking a routine drive along the Thames riverside when he noticed what appeared to be someone sitting with their back against a willow tree gazing out over the Thames. Her dress was torn down the front exposing her breasts.

Shortly after the discovery, a sacking screen was constructed around the body and sightseers were quickly ushered away. The area was soon seething with scenes of crime officers including Detective Superintendent Ted Greeno, head of CID Number One District, Detective Superintendent Woolner, Detective Superintendent James Mitchell (Hammersmith) and Detective Superintendent Bridges.

Detective Superintendent Ted Greeno MBE. Photograph kindly provided by Teddy Greeno and Belinda Greeno, his grandson and granddaughter.

Frederick Grace the field groundsman who lived at the entrance to the riverside walk told the police: *'All I know is there were a lot of cars going down there last night.'* Henry Toms, the caretaker of the field backed up Grace's statement. When pathologist Dr Donald Teare arrived on the scene he conducted a brief examination of the body before ordering its removal to Acton mortuary. There he found two bruise marks on the victim's neck and concluded that she had been manually strangled which had led to asphyxia. Dr Teare estimated that death had taken place between 11.00pm on 16th June and 1.00am on 17th June. After the removal of Figg's body to the mortuary a large team of police officers and Brentford and Chiswick Council employees conducted a fingertip search of a fifty-yard stretch of the river-bank. Soil and grass specimens, dug from under where Figg's body had been dumped, were taken to Scotland Yard's forensic laboratory but unfortunately these yielded no clues. Her shoes, handbag and some jewellery were missing and the police were desperate to recover these in the hope of providing clues.

The inquest into the death of Elizabeth Figg was opened at Ealing Coroner's Court by the coroner Dr Harold Broadbridge, on 18th June and was adjourned until 2nd July after which a further adjournment was ordered until 13th August 1959.

On Thursday 18th June, the day after the discovery of Figg's body, the press published details of the murder and also published a photograph of the victim, which had been taken at the mortuary.

The front page of The Star newspaper of Thursday 18th June 1959. Matchsticks were used to force the victims eyes open at the mortuary. They were removed when the eyes had "set." Ironically, the answer to the question, 'What did Billy Graham see?' was – sexual intercourse taking place in Hyde Park in broad daylight! There had previously been 538 prosecutions in just three months for prostitution and other lewd behaviour in Hyde Park alone. The cost of reproducing The Star/Solo Syndicate Ltd image sponsored by Kate Beal, Talent South Television, Eastleigh, Hampshire.

The victim's photograph was recognised by numerous people who notified the police. The following day Elizabeth's mother Elsie and stepfather George King turned up at Acton Mortuary. Mrs King identified the body as being that of her daughter. (Elsie, maiden name Mort, married James Figg, Elizabeth's father at Wirral, Cheshire in the summer of 1936. Just a few months later their first child Patricia was born. Two years later, on 24th March 1938 Elizabeth arrived and her birth was registered at Wirral. The Figg's marriage gradually soured and they divorced. In 1946 James Figg married Florence Merrick and in 1949 Elsie Figg married George King.)

Just two days before Elizabeth's murder, seventeen-year-old Anne Lewingdon of Ranelagh Gardens, Barnes, was allegedly attacked and almost strangled at Cromwell Road Extension, Chiswick. She had been walking towards home from Turnham Green Station when she was set upon. She fought her attacker who tried to strangle her but escaped and summoned help.

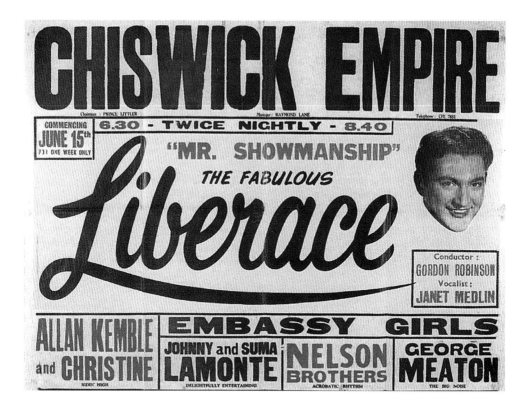

Chiswick Empire: (closing week), 1959. Postcard reproduced by kind permission of Nick Charlesworth, www. vaudeville-postcards.com Nick was at the Empire to see Liberace on Wednesday 17th June 1959. For fifty years he was totally unaware that a murder had been committed close by. Nineteen-year-old Nick and a school friend Christopher Davies, also nineteen had sat in the dress circle where the seats were 10s 6d (fifty two and a half pence), which had increased from 4s 6d (twenty two and a half pence) for the final week. The Empire was the 19th Music Hall to close down in London between 1945 and 1959.

The attacker, described as having *"staring eyes"* was never caught. Did Anne's attacker succeed in his quest two days later with Elizabeth Figg, or were there two monsters lurking in Chiswick? Neither of these girls received justice.

But what's justice? – Liberace knew. Forty-year-old Wladziu Valentino Liberace! He knew and he told his audience all about justice at the Chiswick Empire on Thursday 18th June 1959, the day after the body of Elizabeth Figg had been discovered at Duke's Meadow a short distance away. Wearing his famous gold lamé jacket, Liberace told his enthralled audience: *'It has been said many, many times, ladies and gentlemen, that British justice is the finest in the world. I am absolutely convinced of it now.'* But he wasn't talking about justice for Figg. He was talking about the justice that he claimed he had received that very same day at the High Court in London.

In 1956 the *'Daily Mirror'* had printed a lengthy article implying that the pianist was homosexual. The Mirror's gossip columnist William Connor, writing under the name of *'Cassandra'* had described the entertainer as…*'the summit of sex, the pinnacle of masculine, feminine and neuter. Everything that he, she, and it could ever want…a deadly, winking, sniggering, snuggling, chromium-plated, scent-impregnated, luminous, quivering, fruit-flavoured, mincing, ice-covered heap of mother love.'* Call a spade a spade but not when he's still alive! Liberace sued the paper in the British courts and on Thursday 18th June 1959 he won £ 8,000 damages, (worth approx. £123,000 in 2011), his favourite catchphrase thereafter being: *'I cried all the way to the bank.'* (Ironically, in February 1987 Liberace died of Aids which was believed to have been contracted from homosexual behaviour.) Liberace had been booked to play twice nightly at the Chiswick Empire starting on Monday 15th June and ending on Saturday 20th June.

Throughout the week the police had their work cut out controlling the crowds who had travelled from all over Britain to see their idol. To make matters even more difficult, around thirty student campaigners had besieged the stage door on Wednesday 17th June, protesting the closure of the Empire following Liberace's final performance on Saturday 20th June. Obviously not Liberace fans, the students chanted: *'We want Fatso'* and sang offensive songs. The police needed to be elsewhere on that evening; pursuing the killer of Elizabeth Figg.

The resumed inquest into the death of Figg was held at Ealing Coroner's Court on 13th August before Dr Harold Broadbridge and jury.

Dr Harold George Broadbridge MB, BS, (Lond.) LLB. 11th May 1892 – 4th December 1971. Dr Broadbridge, a GP in North London was admitted to the Middle Temple in October 1938 and was appointed Deputy Coroner for West Middlesex in 1939. He married Nora Milton in 1940 and the following year he was appointed HM Coroner, County of Middlesex Western District. He also held an honours degree in forensic medicine. He was "Called to the Bar" in 1950. Dr Broadbridge had a reputation for kindness and consideration that he showed to the relatives of the deceased that attended his inquest courts. He also had a good rapport with the press.
He retired at the end of March 1965 and lived out his life at Godolphin Road, Weybridge, Surrey. He left a widow, Nora, son Nicholas, and daughter Gillian. Photograph courtesy of Dr Broadbridge's daughter, Gillian Kirk.

Mr Ernest Patrick Forrest, a builder and decorator of Springdale Road, Stamford Hill told the court that he had last seen Figg alive at Holland Park underground station at about 1.10am on the morning of Wednesday 17th June. He said that they had arranged to meet up again at the station at 3.30am but Figg hadn't turned up.

Detective Superintendent James Mitchell told the court: *'We have found no trace of her missing clothes, shoes or jewellery. There is little doubt that she was a prostitute. It looked as though the crime was committed elsewhere, probably in a car because this was her habit.'* Pathologist, Dr Donald Teare said that her scanty clothing did indeed suggest that Figg had been killed elsewhere before being taken to Duke's Meadow. The jury recorded a verdict that *'a person or persons unknown'* had murdered the deceased. Figg, who had died in an undignified manner, was also the recipient of an undignified funeral. She was buried in an unmarked paupers' grave in plot 85 J at Chiswick (New)

Cemetery on 4th September 1959. In the burial records she is described as *"single with no paid employment."* Sadly not one family member or friend attended her funeral.

Figg's body is buried somewhere in the area to the left of the footpath. There is no marker or vase to signify that she had ever existed.

Chapter 4

Another Murder at Chiswick

Let's move on five years, and the Chiswick Empire, which unlike Figg *"died with dignity"* on Liberace's final night, is now just a memory after being demolished and replaced with the office block known as Empire House. Figg's murder was still unsolved and by then Gwynneth Rees and Hannah Tailford had been found dead under suspicious circumstances. Surely, the police must have been concerned that there was a possibility that all three women were murdered and that the killer was the same person – and still at large? The strong link in all three deaths was the River Thames and prostitutes; but believing something and proving it is a different matter.

Any lingering doubts by the police were soon erased, when on Wednesday 8th April 1964 just over two months after Tailford's demise, the body of yet another prostitute was discovered naked and with teeth missing.

Modern photograph of the foreshore at Corney Reach, Chiswick, where Lockwood was found dead by Sergeant Robert Powell of the Thames River Police.

Irene Charlotte Lockwood a twenty-six-year-old blonde who lived at 16 Denbigh Road, Notting Hill, London, was found on the Thames foreshore at Corney Reach, Chiswick, near where Figg's body was found in 1959 and just 300 yards upstream from the spot where Tailford's body had been discovered.

Shortly after Lockwood's body was discovered she was identified by a tattoo on one of her arms. It said: In Memoriam, John. Another tattoo was an image of a crucifix.

Police look on after the body of Irene Lockwood had been placed in a coffin on top of the wall shown in previous photograph. Detective Superintendent Ted Greeno is second from the right. The cost of reproducing this Mirrorpix photograph sponsored by Garvin Gough, freshly cooked food and fine ales, Commercial Hotel, Market Street, Abertillery.

The murder squad detectives who set up HQ at Shepherds Bush police station believed that Lockwood had been drowned, possibly in a bath and then dumped in the Thames. It must now seem certain that a serial killer was at work. Lockwood's body was conveyed to Acton mortuary where pathologist Dr Donald Teare carried out a post-mortem.

On Friday 10th April the inquest into the death of Lockwood was opened in Ealing. An auburn-haired woman (Maureen Gallagher) was allowed by the coroner, Dr Harold Broadbridge, to give her name and address in writing before giving formal evidence of identification of the deceased. She said that she had known Lockwood as Sandra Russell of 16 Denbigh Road, Notting Hill. The inquest was adjourned until 8th May.

On Thursday 16th April the police made a public appeal for information about the last movements of Lockwood who usually frequented Church Street Kensington, and Charing Cross Station. They said she always wore the same clothes. These were: A three-quarter-length imitation leopard skin coat, a dark tight-fitting skirt, a pink jumper and knee-length black leather boots.

Lockwood had been born illegitimately to Minnie Lockwood on 29th September 1938 and her birth was registered in East Retford, Nottinghamshire. She had been educated at Walkeringham Secondary Modern School, which she left in 1953. For the next twelve months she worked at Pear Tree Farm, Walkeringham, which was run by her maternal grandfather. Her early teens were unstable and at the age of nineteen she decided to seek her pot of gold and settled in London.

Four months before her twentieth birthday Lockwood gave birth to a son, Stephen Colin but it appears that his birth was not legally registered and he was taken into care. Lockwood's fourteen criminal convictions included five for soliciting, two for insulting behaviour and one for indecency.

On Monday 27th April 1964, just over two weeks after the discovery of Lockwood's body, the fifty-four-year-old caretaker of Holland Park Lawn Tennis Club, Addison Road, West Kensington, London, walked into Notting Hill police station in a highly distressed state and told a detective that he wanted to get something off his chest.

Kenneth Archibald during an interview confessed to killing Irene Lockwood and dumping her body in the River Thames.

Kenneth Archibald. Artwork by Aran Brown, Abertillery Comprehensive School. © 2011, Aran Brown.

The police should have been jubilant believing the serial killer had handed himself in without a fight. But they weren't. Something wasn't adding up. Archibald wasn't confessing to the earlier murder of Hannah Tailford but the police were convinced that the same person had killed Tailford and Lockwood.

Nevertheless, Archibald on his own confession was charged with the murder of Irene Lockwood and was remanded in custody to appear before Acton Magistrates' Court on Friday 1st May 1964. On Thursday 30th April the police stepped up their inquiries with a special conference which was convened at Scotland Yard.

Daily Mirror

3d.   Friday, May 1, 1964   ●   No. 18,774

Caretaker faces court today

NUDE IN RIVER— MURDER CHARGE

By TOM TULLETT and NORMAN LUCAS

A 54-YEAR-OLD caretaker was charged last night with the murder of Irene Lockwood — the tattooed nude found dead on the Thames foreshore three weeks ago.

The accused man—Kenneth Archibald, of Addison-road, Kensington —will appear in court at Acton this morning.

He had been at Shepherd's Bush police station since late on Monday night.

Irene Lockwood's naked body was found on the north shore of the Thames at Duke's Meadow, Chiswick, on April 18

She was a 26-year-old blonde who came to London from her native Lincolnshire six years ago.

Elegant

She became a prostitute and was known as Sandra Russell.

Shortly before her death she was living in an elegantly-furnished four-room flat at Denbigh-road, Notting Hill, where she paid £12 10s.-a-week rent.

When her body was found, one of the factors leading to her quick identification was the tattoo on her arm.

It said: "In Memoriam, John." The words were enclosed in a circle of flowers. A crucifix was also tattooed on the arm.

A post mortem revealed that her body had been in the river.

Last night, detectives investigating the deaths of three women, whose naked bodies have been found in or near the Thames, stepped up their inquiries. A special conference was called at Scotland Yard.

It was presided over by Deputy Commander Ernest Millen.

For over an hour, the detectives examined and discussed 120 statements. The statements were volunteered after the Yard issued an appeal for information on Tuesday morning.

The detectives are working in three separate squads.

HER SIGHT IS SAVED

A PRETTY blonde sits on a garden bench on a sunny spring day and looks at the flowers.

The peaceful setting is misleading. For the girl in the picture, this is a moment of sheer excitement.

She is beauty queen Rosemary Williams, whose sight has been saved by surgeons.

Rosemary, 19, had an operation eight weeks ago for the removal of a tumour which had made her blind in the left eye and impaired the vision of the other.

For three days after the operation her eyes were covered by bandages.

Yesterday, from the bench in a hospital garden at Belmont Sutton, Surrey, Rosemary saw tulips that had never looked so red.

Next week she hopes to go home to her parents at Plymstock, Devon.

Irene Lockwood, whose naked body was found on the Thames shore.

Star for sale—at a mere £5,000

By MIRROR REPORTER

TOTTENHAM HOT-SPUR shocked the football world last night by putting crack centre forward Bobby Smith on the transfer list.

Smith, who has led the England attack fifteen times, is up for sale at a trifling £5,000.

Lost

This season, 30-year-old Smith has played for England against Wales, the Rest of the World and Ireland.

Then he lost his place in

Spurs' first team and his England place as well.

Johnny Byrne, who plays for West Ham in tomorrow's F A Cup Final, took over as centre-forward for England's latest international against Scotland.

And it is Byrne who is in the England close-season four party.

Bill Nicholson, the manager of Spurs, said last night: "Bobby has given us very good service, and we hope this move will enable him to get another club quickly."

Five other Spurs players have also been put on the transfer list. The whole lot can be bought for £30,000.

Full story—Page 31.

Brooke meets pep-pill kids

By MATTHEW COADY

HOME Secretary Henry Brooke (above) revealed yesterday that he had made a night tour of London's Purple Heart belt with the police.

He told M.Ps. "the thing that impressed itself most deeply on me was the danger to teenagers through the ease of getting Purple Hearts and pep pills."

He gave the Commons no further details of his secret tour.

But, in fact, he spent from 8 p.m. until 4 a.m. on the trail of the kids who live for kicks.

Shocked

He was taken into dingy, smoke-filled basement clubs with dance floors little bigger than table cloths, and what he saw clearly shocked him.

"The future of growing numbers of young people of both sexes is at stake," he told the Commons yesterday.

Mr. Brooke was introducing a Bill which makes it an offence to have pep pills without a prescription or to import them without a licence.

Offenders would be liable to fines of up to £200, or six months' jail OR BOTH.

The drugs broadly covered by the Bill are of the amphetamine type.

Concern

For the most part, M.Ps backed the Bill, but some had reservations.

They argued that it was creating a new offence, and that it allowed the Government to include other drugs if it felt this to be necessary.

On both sides there was general concern for the fate of teenagers.

Back-bench Tory Lord Balniel (Hertford) said the pep-pill craze was an indication that youngsters were finding the real world unrewarding and unconstructive.

Sir Barnett Stross (Lab., Stoke-on-Trent Central), who is a doctor, said: "When I read of youngsters taking twenty, thirty or even forty tablets in a day or two I am horrified.

"I tremble when I think

Continued on Back Page

Front page of the Daily Mirror on 1st May 1964. © Mirrorpix.

It was presided over by Deputy Commander Ernest Millen. The following day when Kenneth Archibald appeared in court, crowds of onlookers, many clutching shopping bags, awaited his arrival; but the police who had covered his head with a blanket, quickly whisked him into the building. In the dock, stocky, grey-haired Archibald stood staring straight ahead, his hands tightly gripping the dock rail. He wore an open-necked white shirt and a grey-brown striped suit.

Giving evidence of Archibald's arrest, Detective Superintendent Frank Davies of F Division CID said: *'On Wednesday 8th April this year at 3.00pm, I saw the dead body of a woman at Acton mortuary. A post-mortem examination showed that she had died from drowning. Later the body was identified as that of Irene Charlotte Lockwood. On Monday 27th April, the defendant presented himself voluntarily at Notting Hill police station and made a verbal statement. He was brought to me at Shepherds Bush police station where I saw him. I saw him again later and took a statement under caution, which is in fact an admission. At 6.45pm last night at Shepherds Bush police station he was charged with the murder of the girl Lockwood.'*

Detective Superintendent Frank Davies. Artwork by Tomas Jones, Brynmawr Foundation School. © 2011, Tomas Jones. The cost of reproducing this artwork sponsored by Sara Wilson, Abertillery.

The Chairman of the Bench asked Archibald if he had anything to say but he just shook his head and remained silent. After the Clerk of the Court told the Bench that Archibald was *"a man of no means,"* he was granted legal aid and was remanded in custody to appear again before Acton Magistrates' Court on Friday 15th May 1964.

On that date at Acton, Archibald was alleged to have murdered Irene Lockwood on the night of 7th April 1964 after they had met at The Windmill public house near the police station at Chiswick High Road. (The police station is now Carrvosso's Restaurant.)

Mr Oliver Nugent prosecuting, told magistrates that the case against Archibald rested solely on his own confession to the police three weeks after the discovery of Lockwood's body. He said the victim had been identified by her fingerprints even though she had been living under the assumed name of Sandra Russell in a £12.10s.0d. a week flat at

Denbigh Road, Notting Hill.

He said that the telephone number of the tennis club where Archibald had worked as a caretaker was found amongst Lockwood's possessions at her flat.

Detective Constable David Bretton told the court that on 9th April he had visited the suspect at his flat at the tennis club at Addison Road, Kensington. He said the visit was the day after the discovery of Lockwood's body and he had told Archibald that he was making inquiries into the death of Irene Lockwood. He said he had shown him a photograph of her but Archibald said he had never heard of her or seen her. DC Bretton said that he had told the suspect that, in Lockwood's diary was the name *"Kenny"* and on a business card was the tennis club telephone number. This was met with the reply: *'My name is Kenneth; a lot of people call me Ken.'* Regarding the card, Archibald had said that he and a man by the name of Cannon had run an *"after hours"* drinking club in his flat at the tennis club but it was Cannon who had the cards printed with the club telephone number. When Bretton had told Archibald that the card had been found at Lockwood's flat, he said: *'I didn't give it to her. I never had any of the cards.'*

Nineteen-year-old Maureen Gallagher of King's Road, Chelsea, said that at one time she had resided with Lockwood at her elegantly-furnished four-roomed flat at Denbigh Road, Notting Hill, knowing that she was a prostitute. When asked who the *"Kenny"* referred to in Lockwood's diary was, she replied: *'He is young looking, about twenty-four, 5ft 11 ins tall, with sleek straight dark hair and well dressed.'* Surely she should have said: *'He looked about sixty years of age, was short, overweight, with grey hair'.* Something not quite right here. Or were there two men called *"Kenny?"*

Detective Constable Stanley Moorehead of Notting Hill CID told the court that on 27th April 1964 he had received a telephone call from Archibald complaining that the storeroom had been broken into at the Addison Road Tennis Club. Later that same day Archibald had walked into Notting Hill police station saying he wanted to hand himself in. Moorehead said he believed that Archibald had meant he was giving himself up for the club store break-in, but when asked if he was admitting to stealing property from the tennis club he replied: *'No, I pushed the girl in the river…. You know, the blonde, Lockwood, at Chiswick.'* Detective Constable Thomas Ferguson, also of Notting Hill CID told the court that Archibald had said in his presence at Notting Hill police station: *'I killed that girl Lockwood; you know the one in the photograph that was shown to me…. I had been drinking. I met her in a pub at Chiswick just before closing time. We went down to the river and there was a row and I strangled her. After that I pushed her into the river down a ramp.'* DC Ferguson alleged that when interrogated, Archibald had claimed he had lost his temper with Lockwood because she insisted on payment before sex took place. He said he strangled her, stripped her and then rolled her body into the river and then took her clothes home to burn.

The police had taken Archibald to Chiswick where he had identified The Windmill public house where he alleged he had been with Lockwood on the night of the murder. Mr John Rankin, the joint licensee of The Windmill, 214 Chiswick High Road, told the court that he recognised a photograph of Lockwood who had frequented the pub on a number of occasions with a man about thirty years of age. But he was insistent that on 7th April, the night of her murder, Lockwood was alone in The Windmill drinking spirits. He said he did not remember ever seeing Archibald, concluding with the words: *'I would definitely have recognised anyone she had met that night.'*

The hearing was adjourned until Friday 22nd May 1964.

Archibald appeared at Acton Magistrates' Court on that date accused of murdering Irene Lockwood.

Pathologist, Dr Donald Teare, told the court that he found Lockwood had died as a result of drowning. He also found a gash over the right side of the victim's chest was caused after her death. Unfortunately, he had also found that two lives were snuffed out at the time Lockwood was murdered, as she had been about four months pregnant. Dr Teare told the court: *'I have been acquainted with the statement allegedly made by Archibald that he strangled, stripped and rolled the girl down to the river. Nothing in my findings was inconsistent with that account.... I think it likely that one would find abrasions as a result of this treatment. I think it would be likely but not certain. I could not find any abrasions or marks.'*

The Windmill portacabin as it looked on the night Irene Lockwood was killed in April 1964. The temporary cabin had been erected in 1962 in front of the old public house, which was then demolished to make way for the new premises, which is seen here under construction. When the new building was completed in 1965, the cabin was removed and The Windmill occupied part of the ground floor. In the mid 1990s it was renamed Jack Stamp's Beerhouse but is now Balans Restaurant. Photograph courtesy of Chiswick Local Studies Library. The cost of reproducing this photograph sponsored by Jack Edwards, Roseheyworth, Abertillery.

After answering questions put to him by Archibald's solicitor Mr Edward Hume, Dr Teare then left the witness box. The court decided that Archibald should stand trial for the murder of Lockwood and the chairman, Major Charles Fisher told the defendant that he would be further remanded in custody to stand trial at the Old Bailey. (Major Fisher, 1895-1987 was a former Deputy Lieutenant of Middlesex and High Sheriff of London.) During a six-day trial that ended on 23rd June 1964 Archibald changed his guilty plea and then denied having anything to do with Lockwood's murder. Mr EJP Cussen for the prosecution explained to the jury that Irene Lockwood generally carried on her profession as a prostitute in Bayswater and Notting Hill, but sometimes moved further afield. On the night of her murder she found herself drinking until closing time in The Windmill public house on Chiswick High Road.

After leaving the pub Lockwood had led Archibald down (Devonshire Road and Church Street) to the slipway of the Thames where intercourse was expected to take place for a fee of £4. There was a disagreement about payment and Archibald in a temper seized her by the throat and strangled her before removing her clothing and rolling her body into the river. Cussen, related: *'When detectives went to the deceased's address they found a visiting card bearing the name "Kenny" and the telephone number Park 7157. The defendant was known as "Kenny" and the telephone number was that of the tennis club where he had a part-time job as a caretaker. Shown a photograph of the dead woman, [by the police] Archibald had said: "I have never seen her in my life." Three weeks later on 27th April the defendant went to Notting Hill police station of his own accord.'* Cussen then said that Archibald had told the police: *'I killed the girl Lockwood. You know, the girl in the photo that was shown to me. After the row over payment I strangled Lockwood who neither screamed nor made a noise. I pushed her against a wall and she fell to the ground. It was then that I made the decision to strip her and roll her body into the Thames. I then took the girl's clothes home and burned them.'* Over a five-day period a steady stream of witnesses gave their evidence.

The slipway to the Thames at Church Street, Chiswick.

On the last day of the trial when Archibald walked into the dock to give evidence he was wearing a hearing aid and appeared very nervous. He told the jury that on the morning of 27th April 1964 a room at the tennis club was broken into and cash and stock was taken. Later that morning he had appeared at Marlborough Street Magistrates' Court accused of stealing a hearing aid from a hearing aid specialist. He had pleaded guilty to that charge but the magistrates refused to accept the plea and insisted that he plead not guilty. After the hearing had been adjourned he went to The Colville public house in Notting Hill and had six beers and then went to Notting Hill police station in the afternoon where he falsely claimed that he had killed Irene Lockwood. When he was asked why he made the statement he replied: *'I was fed up and mixed up and so I decided to confess to the murder. I was worried at the thought of losing my job, my flat, and forfeiting my service and disability pension.'*

After retiring and considering their verdict for forty minutes the jury returned to a packed and hushed courtroom. When asked in the usual formula if they had reached a verdict, the jury foreman replied: *'Yes.'* When asked if the jury had found Kenneth Archibald guilty or not guilty of the murder of Irene Charlotte Lockwood he replied: *'Not guilty.'* With that verdict returned Mr Justice Nield ordered that Archibald be released.

On leaving court Archibald told the press: *'I cannot get away from this building quickly enough. Now I have to look for a new job and somewhere to live. You see I have lost my job at the tennis club and the flat that went with it. I shall never confess to anything again. The reason I confessed to this murder, which I did not do, was because I was terribly depressed, confused and fed up. I suppose if I hadn't had six beers that day I would never have walked into Notting Hill police station that day and confessed.'*

An unsettling feature of Archibald's confession was that certain details which were known only to the killer and the police, apparently fitted in perfectly. Some people have questioned whether the police had coerced Archibald to *"volunteer"* information that prior to his visit to Notting Hill, he knew nothing about. If the jury had believed Archibald's original confession and found him guilty of the murder of Irene Lockwood he may have been hanged. Just two months after his acquittal the very last hangings took place in Britain before the practice was abolished.

Was Archibald just a *"loner"* seeking attention, or was he and one or more of his cronies at his *"after hours"* drinking club involved in the nudes' murders?

He told the press after his acquittal that he was going to leave London. And pigs might fly! Archibald, who had been born in Sunderland, Durham, Tyne and Wear in 1910 died at Flat 6, 40 Coleman Road, Southwark, London, on 20th October 1972. This was just six miles away from his former flat. The cause of death was fibrocalcific aortic stenosis. He was cremated at Honor Oak Crematorium, Forest Hill, London, on Tuesday 31st October 1972. Archibald had married Nada Nathan at Holderness in the East Riding of Yorkshire in 1941, but the marriage had failed after five years. He had left the army in 1947 with the rank of sergeant having served his country in France.

Irene Lockwood's inquest had been formally opened at Ealing on 10th April 1964 and adjourned until 8th May.

Oddly, there are no reports in the Chiswick or Ealing newspapers about the resumed inquest. It can only be assumed that the verdict into her death would have been: *'Murder by a person or persons unknown.'* Irene Charlotte Lockwood was buried in a paupers' grave in plot 70 J at Chiswick (New) Cemetery on 9th July 1964. Two sets of burial records exist for her. In life she used many aliases. In death, she is named in one record book as Sandra Lockwood and in another as Sandra Russell.

Chapter 5

A Miscarriage of Justice?

Regardless of Archibald's earlier confession on 27th April to the murder of Irene Lockwood, the search for the nudes' killer had already intensified. Three days before his confession at Notting Hill, the body of another prostitute, twenty-two-year-old Helene Catherine Barthelemy of 34 Talbot Road Harlesden, London was found naked by Mr Clark May in a lane outside the rear garden of his home at 199 Boston Manor Road, Brentford.

The lane at the rear of Boston Manor Road, Brentford where the body of Barthelemy was found. A tarpaulin cover hides the body from public view.

She was undoubtedly another victim of the *"Stripper."* The spot where she was found was accessed by a lane off Swyncombe Avenue, Brentford and was just a mile or so from the locations where the previous four bodies were found. Barthelemy, a petite brunette was found to have had four of her teeth removed but there was no indication that a blow had dislodged them. Owing to a lack of blood in the gums it appeared that they had been extracted after her death.

Helene Catherine Barthelemy was born on 9th June 1941 to Maurice and Mary Barthelemy at Ormiston, East Lothian, sixteen miles from Edinburgh. Little is known of her early life but by 1957 she was living in Blackpool.

Helene Barthelemy on Blackpool Promenade circa 1957-59. Photograph kindly provided by Thomas James Barthelemy, son of Helene.

On 7th October 1960 she gave birth to a baby son, Thomas James Barthelemy and registered his birth in Littleboro', Rochdale, Lancashire. His father was named as Kenneth Ferguson who was employed as a cotton feeder. Ferguson however was not the father and sadly Helene gave Thomas up for adoption.

(On Wednesday 8th July 2009, forty-nine-year-old Thomas contacted the author. He said he became aware of his mother's murder when he was seventeen. At the age of twenty-one he was given a file regarding his mother's life and murder. Thomas spent a lot of time and money hiring private investigators to unravel his and his mother's past. He was able to trace his real father who had died on 5th November 1973 and at the end of 2008 he met his half sister, his father's daughter not his mother's. Thomas has a son twenty-seven, a son twenty-five, and a daughter aged twenty-one. He and his wife also adopted a five-year-old boy in 2005.)

On Monday 8th October 1962 Barthelemy, living in Blackpool but of no fixed abode and described as a former striptease artiste, appeared at Liverpool Assizes charged with robbing with aggravation Friend Taylor aged twenty-five, who lived in Oldham, Greater Manchester. He had been staying in Blackpool on holiday. Barthelemy had allegedly lured Taylor to the sand dunes at Squires Gate, Blackpool on Friday 27th July 1962 where three male accomplices lay in wait. The thugs gave Taylor a severe beating and stole his wallet containing £22.5s.0d. He staggered to the road and a passing motorist conveyed him to hospital, where eighteen stitches were inserted in a face wound. The assailants were never identified and during a three day trial Barthelemy protested her innocence, claiming Taylor had been mistaken in his identity of her.

Helene posing on the sand hills at Blackpool circa 1963. Photograph kindly provided by Thomas James Barthelemy, son of Helene.

Mr Brian Duckworth for the Crown said that on 27th July that year Mr Taylor met Barthelemy and spent two hours with her on the pleasure beach. At around 8.00pm that evening they met up again and went to The Huntsman Hotel and later ended up on the sand dunes at Squires Gate. He said that Taylor took off his coat and jacket and he and the defendant lay down in the sand. After a few minutes Taylor felt a pebble hit him so he got up and saw three men running towards him. Taylor was beaten and kicked in the stomach and left lying on the sand. Taylor then heard the defendant shout: *'Stop it Jock. He has had enough.'* Duckworth continued that this remark indicated that the defendant knew the three men and indeed, when Taylor and Barthelemy were on Blackpool Promenade earlier in the evening, Taylor heard one of the same three say to her that he would see her later. When questioned the following day, Barthelemy told the police that it could not have been her as she had been with a man to the Rendezvous Cinema in Bond Street, on the night of the alleged attack to see the film *"El Cid."* (The 1961 historical epic starring Charlton Heston and Sophia Loren.)

Regardless of her alibi, Friend Taylor picked Barthelemy out at an identity parade the day after the robbery. Duckworth told the Liverpool Assizes: *'This is a case of a young girl acting in league with three men, who together conceived a plan that she should lure someone onto the sand hills, and while there the men would set about him and rob him.'* With those words the trial was adjourned until the following day.

When the hearing resumed Friend Taylor who was described in court as a man of complete integrity, gave evidence that Barthelemy had been with him when the three men attacked him. He said: '*I got a blow of some sort across the forehead and blood spurted all over my face. I'm not sure if I was attacked with a knife or a razor. I haven't the slightest doubt that she was the girl with them.*' He also said that he recognised one of the men at the sand hills as one he had seen earlier on the evening of the attack when this person had spoken to the defendant briefly near the Palatine Hotel.

The Rendezvous Cinema at Bond Street, Blackpool, which was crucial to Barthelemy's alibi. The cinema which boasted 1100 seats was built in 1925 and closed in 1972. It was then used as a bingo hall. Photograph courtesy of the Blackpool Gazette.

Two prosecution witnesses, a bingo stall attendant on the Golden Mile, and a waiter at The Huntsman Hotel told the court that they had no doubt that Barthelemy was the same girl that they had seen Friend Taylor with on the day of the alleged robbery.

A view of Blackpool Promenade in the early 1960s. On the right is The Huntsman Hotel where it was alleged that Barthelemy had been drinking with Friend Taylor shortly before robbing him. Photograph courtesy of Blackpool Central Library. The cost of reproducing this photograph sponsored by Chat magazine.

Detective Sergeant HT Jenkins told the court that when he had questioned the accused about the robbery she told him it could not possibly have been her as she had been to the Rendezvous Cinema that evening with a friend by the name of David Graham and in fact had spoken to the manager as she had gone into the cinema. DS Jenkins said that when he charged Barthelemy she had said to him: *'What can I say to convince you?'*

The cinema manager Walter Worsley next gave evidence for the prosecution. He said that he had indeed seen the accused outside the cinema with a young man in July, but not on 27th July but 26th. He said that on the 27th he was busy in his office from 6.30pm until 8.30pm so the defendant could not possibly have spoken to him that evening as she had claimed.

If this evidence wasn't enough to drop Barthelemy in it, she then went on to hang herself. She told the court that early in 1962 she had been a striptease artiste on the Golden Mile but left that job to work as a prostitute. She said that in July, the month of the alleged robbery, she met *four* lads from the Preston area and one of them asked her what she did for a living. When she told him that she was a prostitute one of the lads asked her if she fancied *"rolling a punter"* to which she had replied: *'No. It is not in my line.'* She said that on the day of the alleged attack she had been to the hairdresser's between 2.00 and 3.15pm. She then went to the funfair near Central Station and met up with a friend, David Graham. She stayed at the fair until about 5.00 – 5.30pm but met again with Graham at 7.30pm and they went together to the Rendezvous Cinema where she had acknowledged the cinema manager. She had stayed in the cinema with David Graham until the end of the screening.

Mr John Ward defending (instructed by Mr Ian Collins) asked Barthelemy what she did after leaving the cinema to which she replied that she had *"gone on the game."* She said: *'I went to Stanley Park with a client and we parted about 11.00pm, then I went with another client until about 11.30pm after which I then went with another man before heading for an all-night café.'*

Duckworth, prosecuting asked the defendant what she understood *"rolling a punter"* to mean, to which she replied: *'Putting my hand in a man's pocket and taking his wallet.'* She went on to say that she had never seen any of the four men before their chance meeting in July and had not seen them since. She said she had never seen Friend Taylor before her arrest. She said: *'He is definitely mistaken.'* In further cross-examination by Duckworth she denied going to a different hairdresser the day after the robbery to try to change her appearance. The case was adjourned until the following day. The final day of the trial took place on 10th October. Oldham victim Friend Taylor, who by then was living at Fordway Avenue, Blackpool, was in court. David Graham, Barthelemy's friend told the hushed court that he himself was awaiting sentence for larceny. He said he had met Barthelemy at about 6.30pm on Friday 27th July near the *"waltzer"* in the fairground at Bonny Street. He said he accompanied her to the Rendezvous Cinema where they watched *"El Cid"* and they stayed to the end, after which he took her in his van to Chapel Street. Mr Brian Duckworth prosecuting asked Graham if he had signed a police statement at South King Street police station to the effect that he was not in the company of Barthelemy on the night in question. He replied that he had signed the statement but it was forced out of him by *"physical violence"* at the police station.

Duckworth then asked Graham: *'You do agree that the essence of the statement is in complete contradiction of what you have said on oath today? Which is true?'* Graham replied: '*What I have said today. Some of the words in my police statement were put into my mouth by the police.*' After other inconsequential evidence was given, the jury retired to consider their verdict. They returned after deliberating for one hour and forty minutes and told the court that they had found the defendant guilty of robbery with aggravation with three persons unknown and not guilty of a charge of unlawful wounding.

Mr Justice Stable was informed that Barthelemy had been convicted at Liverpool Magistrates' Court in March 1962 for assisting in the management of a brothel for which she had been fined £20. Regarding the case of robbery with aggravation of which she had just been convicted the judge asked Barthelemy if she had anything to say.

She nervously replied: '*I have done my best to prove my innocence.*' Mr Justice Stable told her: '*The jury has found you guilty of an absolutely appalling crime of decoying a young man into the sand dunes to be set upon by three blackguards [scoundrels]. The only way of stopping this sort of thing is to make it not worthwhile. You will go to prison for four years.*' Barthelemy, after gazing at the judge for a few seconds fainted and had to be carried from the dock by two female prison officers. When she revived she was led down the iron staircase to the cells.

On Monday 4th February 1963, Barthelemy appeared at the Court of Criminal Appeal in London to fight her conviction four months previously. Mr James Comyn, QC, submitted to the three judges at the appeal hearing that the verdict at Liverpool Assizes was unsafe. It was revealed that Friend Taylor the man who had allegedly been robbed and beaten on the sand dunes at Blackpool was not as squeaky clean as was made out in court in October 1962. There he had been described as a man of complete integrity. It now transpired that Taylor, in 1951 and 1952 had appeared before juvenile courts for theft. In 1955 he had appeared before Worthing magistrates for theft and at Blackpool in March 1959, he was placed on probation, again for theft. At Lytham in December 1959 he had been jailed for nine months for the theft of £40 and in April 1961 he was jailed for twelve months for housebreaking.

(One wonders where Taylor got the £22.5s.0d in the first place, of which he was allegedly robbed - poetic justice?)

Mr Brian Duckworth for the Crown who had previously prosecuted Barthelemy at Liverpool Assizes told the appeal court: '*I am bound to concede that this does place a different aspect on the case, but it does not follow that if a man has previous convictions he has not told the truth on a subsequent occasion. He was in the company of a young woman for five hours that Friday. [27th July 1962] He was not picking up a prostitute in a back street. He spent two hours on the front with her in the full light of day. In the evening he had drinks with her in a hotel, and later went to the sand dunes with her. Any young man in those circumstances would have no doubt about identifying the girl the next day.*'

After discussing at length various aspects of the case with his fellow judges, Mr Justice Ashworth one of the three appeal court judges addressing the court said: '*Had the defence counsel [at Liverpool Assizes] known about Taylor's convictions at the trial he would have had no compunction in putting them to Taylor because Barthelemy as a known prostitute had only one previous conviction – in connection with running a brothel. In such a case as the present where it might be said to be touch-and-go which way the jury's decision might go, the addition of these facts regarding the victim's record of dishonesty might well have swayed the jury to acquit this appellant. It is sufficient for this court to say that they might have done so. On the ground that the fresh evidence might have produced a different verdict, the conviction will be quashed.'* They may as well have sentenced Barthelemy to death. If she had lost the appeal she would still have been safely behind bars when her killer was prowling the streets of west London, stalking victim number five. The Bible book of Ecclesiastes chapter 9 v11 correctly states: *'...time and unforeseen occurrence befall them all.'* Barthelemy ended up in the wrong place at the wrong time. Brentford, London. Friday 24th April 1964. Naked and dead!

Helene had so desired the bright lights of London. It is ironic that she should die in the shadows. In the words of the Peter and Gordon song which reached number one in the charts in the month she was murdered, she died in *'A World Without Love.'*

A murder squad had been established at Brentford under the command of Detective Superintendent Maurice Osborn of Scotland Yard.

Detective Superintendent Maurice Osborn. Artwork provided by Tomas Jones, Brynmawr Foundation School. © 2011, Tomas Jones. The cost of reproducing this artwork sponsored by Kiowa Edwards, Abertillery.

The squad worked closely with three other murder squads; the ones dealing with the deaths of Rees, Tailford and Lockwood. All four squads kept in mind the unsolved murder of Figg. They also bore in mind the possibility that the deaths of all five women may be linked, and that there could be more than one killer.

The inquest into the death of Barthelemy opened at Ealing on Monday 27th April 1964. Barthelemy's mother, Mary Thompson of Grimsby told the coroner Dr Harold Broadbridge that she had last seen her daughter alive in 1960. After pathologist Dr Donald Teare said that the cause of death was asphyxia caused by pressure on the neck; the inquest was adjourned until 4th June 1964.

On that date it was again adjourned - until 2nd November 1964. Barthelemy was buried on 16th September 1964 in a paupers' grave at Chiswick (New) Cemetery. She was interred in plot 70 J which was the same common grave that Irene Lockwood had been buried in just over two months earlier. An unknown person paid the £4.1s.0d burial fee. Elizabeth Figg was buried in plot 85 J just a few steps away. (See page 32)

On 2nd November 1964, Dr Harold Broadbridge sat with an all male jury at Ealing Town Hall. Mr Clark May, a horticulturist of 199 Boston Manor Road, Brentford, told the inquest that he had gone into his back garden at 7.15am on the morning of 24th April. He said he found the body of Barthelemy lying in the service lane at the rear of his house. He said he had been in the lane at 7.30pm the previous evening and the body was not there then and he had not noticed any unusual noises during the night.

Pathologist Dr Donald Teare said: *'The naked body of the girl was very dirty and had been dead for about two days. Marks on her back showed she had been wearing her underclothes when she had died. The throat was bruised and had some abrasions. Marks on the throat showed she had probably been wearing a roll-neck collar at the time of her death.'* Detective Superintendent Maurice Osborn told the inquest: *'We haven't discovered who the assailant was or when the girl died. She was identified through her fingerprints.... We could find none of her clothing, only a handbag at a jazz club used by coloured people.'* [The Jazz Cub, 207 Westbourne Road, Notting Hill.] *'Most of her clients were white men, but she associated with coloured people quite a lot, probably drug addicts. We know she smoked Indian hemp herself.'* Dr Broadbridge then told the jury: *'The police are up against a brick wall. They have done everything possible to trace the people responsible but without success. There is no point in holding up this inquest any longer, although the police will continue to do their best to find the assailants.'* After retiring to consider their verdict, the foreman of the jury of ten men told the coroner that they found that *'a person or persons unknown'* had murdered Barthelemy.

Following Barthelemy's demise, Scotland Yard had put out an urgent appeal to all women involved in the sex trade. They said: *'All the dead women usually picked up clients from streets or clubs in the central and west London area and often went with them in vehicles. Inquiries on these lines by the murder teams have brought to light cases where women have been persuaded to enter cars and then forced to strip under threat of violence and in one case under threat of a knife. In some cases violence has actually been used and the women concerned are fortunate not to have been killed. Police fear that if information is not forthcoming yet another prostitute may be found dead. This appeal is urgently directed to all those women whose means of livelihood place them in danger of meeting the same fate.'* Right then, that should put a stop to it. – No chance!

Chapter 6

A Third Murder at Chiswick

At 5.00am on Tuesday 14th July 1964, less than three months after Barthelemy's murder, another prostitute's naked body was discovered in a sitting position at the entrance to a private lock-up garage at 48 Berrymede Road, Acton Green, Chiswick, London. She had been strangled and a number of her teeth were missing. The finder was Mr George Heard aged thirty-four, a chauffeur of 53 Berrymede Road.

George Heard in shirtsleeves standing near the garage double doors where Fleming's body had been dumped. The cost of reproducing this Mirrorpix photograph sponsored by Blaenau Gwent County Borough Council and UK Steel Enterprise Limited.

Looking out of his house window he noticed what he thought was a tailor's dummy at the entrance to the garage belonging to Mr Owen Jones at number 48, which was directly opposite number 53. He told the police: *'I went over there and found it was the body of a woman. She was naked. She was sort of cross-legged with arms folded and her head slumped forward. There was no sign of her clothes. There were marks on the body as though she had been in the boot of a car. I was awoken between 2.00 and 3.00am by a car reversing, but I didn't take any notice because cars often come down here not knowing it is a blocked-up [dead end] road.'* George's wife Doreen aged thirty-four told the police that at first she also thought the body was a tailor's dummy. A number of residents of Berrymede Road later told the police that they had heard a noisy vehicle enter and leave the quiet cul-de-sac in the early hours of the morning of the discovery of the body, but could give no further details. Night shift decorators working in the rear of premises at Chiswick High Road one and a half miles from Berrymede Road told police about things that they had seen and heard in the Chiswick High Road service lane two hours prior to the discovery of the body. They said that around 3.00am they heard a vehicle reverse into the lane and heard car doors slamming. Looking through the window they saw a man at the side of the vehicle and when he realised that he was being watched he hurriedly drove away. They said it was too dark to get a description of the man but were sure that the vehicle was either an estate car or a small van.

Mary Fleming 1933-1964. Artwork based on a damaged photograph of Fleming by Aran Brown, Abertillery Comprehensive School. © 2011, Aran Brown.

The body found was later identified as being that of mother of four, thirty-year-old Mary Fleming of 44 Lancaster Road, Notting Hill, London. She had last been seen alive at about midnight on 10th July soliciting in Queensway. It was believed that she had been wearing a green-grey two-piece costume and was carrying a black-and-tartan handbag with a long strap. In the bag was a National Assistance book, number 13/13978178, and a Family Allowance book, number 7125646. None of Fleming's clothes or her bag were ever found.

Daily Mirror

3d. Wednesday, July 15, 1964 + No. 18,838

Police warn: 'He will strike again'

NUDE No 5— RIVER KILLER HUNTED

The Home Secretary and the gangsters

AN evil criminal gang, the like of which London has never known before, is defying Scotland Yard and growing fat on the proceeds of extortion and intimidation.

This gang is so rich, powerful and ruthless that the police are unable to crack down on it.

Victims are too terrified to go to the police. Witnesses are too scared to tell their story in court. Or they tell the wrong story. Or they go dumb or go missing because they have been bribed or threatened.

SAFEGUARD

MPs are alarmed about these dangerous gangsters. Home Secretary Henry Brooke faces questions in the Commons tomorrow on police inquiries and reports about protection money racketeers, blackmail and intimidation.

The police, who know what is happening, but cannot pin any evidence on the villains, are hamstrung.

In a free country there must certainly be every safeguard to protect the rights of people who are suspected and questioned by the police.

But there is little wonder that the police are increasingly frustrated when, more and more, these safeguards allow villainy to flourish unchecked.

JUSTICE

If the police are powerless to bring the gang to justice, Parliament must decide what extra powers are needed to break up this growing empire of London gangsterdom.

It must be smashed quickly before the capital is completely enmeshed in a network of organised racketeering,

Continued on Page Two

By BARRY STANLEY

ONE of Scotland Yard's biggest manhunts was launched yesterday to find a sex-crazed killer who has murdered five women in eight months.

The "carbon-copy" murderer's fifth nude victim was named last night as Glasgow-born prostitute Mary Fleming, 31.

Her body was found slumped in a quiet London cul-de-sac yesterday. She had been strangled.

Strangled

The murder was exactly like the killing in April of prostitute Helen Barthelemy.

Her body was discovered in a "lovers' alley" three miles from the spot where Mary Fleming was found yesterday.

Both girls had been strangled. And both had been killed away from the spots where they were found.

And Scotland Yard's top murder detectives think that both girls were dumped from the same car.

Mary Fleming—a slim brunette—had been dead at least twenty-four hours when her body was found in Berrymede-road, Acton Green, Chiswick.

She lived in a ground-floor, one-room flat in Lancaster-road, Notting Hill, with her two children—Veronica, 2, and David, 8 months.

Her married name was Fleming, but she also used the name Mary Turner.

Vicious

Scotland Yard detectives are convinced that the killer of Mary Fleming and Helen Barthelemy also murdered three other prostitutes in the past eight months.

The dead women have been found nude in or around the West London reaches of the Thames.

All London's police have been told: "This vicious killer must be found quickly—before he strikes again."

Detectives want to interview anyone who may have seen Mary Fleming walking along Queensway Bayswater, early on Saturday.

Mary Fleming she was found strangled.

KIDNAPPED CAT COMES HOME

MICKEY, the cat held for £1,000 ransom by kidnappers, drank cream from his silver bowl at home last night.

He is pictured above getting a welcome-home kiss from his owner, Miss Doris Easton.

Miss Easton, 60, burst into tears when an old-age pensioner walked in—holding Mickey in his arms.

The pensioner, Mr. Robert Channel, 77, collected a £20 reward. He spotted Mickey early yesterday morning when he opened the door of his flat in Murray-grove, Shoreditch, London, to take in his Daily Mirror.

When he started to read the paper, he saw Mickey's picture star-

ing at him from Page Three. Mickey, a 17-year-old ginger tom, was snatched from Miss Easton's flat at her hotel in Belgrave-road, Victoria, on Friday, by kidnappers who later phoned to demand £1,000.

A police spokesman said: "We think the kidnappers must have panicked—and turned Mickey loose."

Front page of the Daily Mirror on 15th July 1964. The cost of reproducing this Mirrorpix image sponsored by Taste of Enterprise, Heads of the Valleys.

53

Little is known about Fleming who was born Mary Theresa Cuthbertson Betty at West Kilpatrick, Dumbarton, Scotland in 1933. Her parents were Richard and Helen Betty and the family soon moved to Barrow-in-Furness, Cumbria. In August 1953, Mary married James Fleming at St Mary's Catholic Church at Barrow-in-Furness.

Three months later she gave birth; either six months premature or she had already been six months pregnant with Michael when she had walked down the aisle. Shortly afterwards her marriage to James Fleming floundered and Mary and baby Michael stayed for a while with her parents. Not long after, she left her mother minding Michael and took work at a restaurant at Biggar Bank, Cumbria. Soon Mary and her mother became embroiled in blazing rows and she stormed out of her parents' home, never to see them or her baby again. In 1956 she gave birth to a son named Robert but failed to register his birth legally. After putting Robert into care she dossed around, eventually finding herself in London. Between 1956 and the time of her death she had accrued a long criminal record for soliciting and for theft. In February 1959, she was jailed for three months for her part in rifling a gas meter at her lodgings in the East End of London. Her takings were £5.3s.0d

In September 1959 she moved into a house in Pembridge Gardens, Kensington, with former Coldstream Guard Michael Turner aged twenty. In April 1962 she gave birth to her third child, a girl and registered the birth under the name of Veronica G Turner. Fleming and Turner were by this time living at Powis Gardens, Notting Hill.

Towards the end of 1963 Mary Fleming gave birth to a fourth child, a boy whom she registered at Paddington under the name of David M Turner. Michael Turner by this time had parted company with Mary and in April 1964, three months before her death, she, Veronica and baby David moved into 25 Geraldine Road, Chiswick.

In May she fled the Geraldine Road property leaving unpaid bills. She and the two children then moved on to her final destination in life; a ground floor, one-room flat at 44 Lancaster Road, Notting Hill.

On Sunday 19th July, five days after the discovery of Fleming's body, Ron Mount of the *'News of the World'* wrote an open letter to the killer to call a halt on the murders. He appealed to him to try to understand the enormity of what he had done and the grief he had caused the victims' families. Did Ron's impassioned plea work? Four and a half months went by after Mary's demise and no more killings. The killer hadn't been apprehended – yet, but at least the killings had stopped. Well done Ron!

But psychopaths don't stop killing because of pity towards their victims or their families. Ron also appealed to the killer to hand himself in to the police. What on earth was going on in Ron's mind? What on earth was going on in the mind of the editor of the *'News of the World'*? The content of the open letter with its explicit details of how the previous prostitutes were murdered more than likely whipped the killer up into a frenzy rather than appealed to his good nature. What Ron hadn't thought through was that whatever kink the killer was afflicted with, he wasn't stupid. If he gave himself up to the police he wouldn't be able to kill again, if he so wished. Added to that, hanging in Britain was still in fashion and the nudes' murderer surely had no desire to be one of the last in Britain to hang.

(That dubious honour went to Peter Anthony Allen aged twenty-one and Gwynne Owen Evans aged twenty-four who were hanged for murdering John Alan West in April 1964. Allen and Evans were hanged simultaneously at 8.00am on 13th August

1964; Allen at Walton Prison Liverpool and Evans at Strangeways Prison Manchester.)

The inquest into the death of Mary Fleming was held at Ealing Coroner's Court on 2nd November 1964 before Dr Harold Broadbridge and a jury of ten men. Fleming's and Barthelemy's inquests were held jointly on that date and the jury's verdict into the death of Fleming was the same as Barthelemy's; *'Murder by a person or persons unknown.'*

Fleming was buried on 3rd November 1964, the day after her inquest in plot number 55362 at Kensal Green Cemetery, Harrow Road, London W10.

Following a series of exhaustive tests by the Metropolitan Police Forensic Laboratory to produce clues that would lead to the apprehension of the serial killer, vital information was gleaned from the bodies of the last two victims, Barthelemy and Fleming. Their bodies were covered with minute dust particles, which under microscopic examination were shown to contain very small particles of paint. It became apparent that both of the victims' bodies had been stored in or near premises where cars had been re-sprayed. It appeared to the police that they were on the verge of ending the killings.

Daily Mirror

4d. Friday, November 27, 1964 ✦ ✦ ✦ No. 18,954

1150

Murder drama of tattooed call girl

NUDE No 6
WAS STEPHEN WARD WITNESS

By TOM TULLETT, Chief of the Mirror Crime Bureau

THE sixth naked girl found murdered in West London was named last night as 23-year-old Margaret McGowan—a prostitute who gave evidence at the Stephen Ward vice trial.

Miss McGowan, whose left arm was heavily tattooed, used at least four other names: Frances Brown, Frances Quinn, Anne Sutherland, Susan Edwards.

She called herself Frances Brown when she gave evidence in the Ward case at the Old Bailey seventeen months ago.

In her evidence, she said that she twice went to Ward's flat with another prostitute-witness — blonde, 20-year-old Vicky Barrett.

Margaret McGowan, born in Glasgow, is now believed to have been strangled before her body was hidden under rubble and a dustbin-lid, in a Civil Defence car park in Hornton-street, Kensington.

Blackmail

Scotland Yard detectives believe she was murdered by the killer of five other prostitutes whose bodies have been discovered during the last year.

One of the previous five victims—22-year-old Helen Barthelemy, found strangled and stripped at Brentford last April—knew several women named in the Ward Case.

She had also been in a photo-blackmail racket with a SEVENTH murdered prostitute—redhaired Vicky Pender, 22, whose killer was jailed for life in July, 1963.

Last night, thirty detectives, who have worked on the six unsolved murders, launched a big drive to catch the killer.

Plain-clothes policewomen joined the hunt. They toured the West End—talking to prostitutes, showing pictures of Margaret McGowan.

Picture

The policewomen concentrated on women who had helped inquiries into the earlier killings.

Scotland Yard issued a picture of Margaret McGowan, to be passed to all police forces and be shown on television.

A Yard spokesman said: "We appeal to anyone who knows the girl, or has seen her, or knows of her movements in the past eight weeks, to come forward."

Detectives have found that Miss McGowan worked as a prostitute in the Bayswater - Kensington - Notting Hill areas—also frequented by four of the five earlier murder victims.

These four were Helen Barthelemy, Hannah Tailford, 30, Irene Lockwood, 29, and Mrs. Mary Fleming, 30.

The other murdered prostitute was 22-year-old Gwynneth Rees.

THIS was Margaret McGowan at the time of the Stephen Ward trial.

Big factories switch plan to beat crisis

By VICTOR KNIGHT and WILLIAM WOLFF

BEAT-THE-CRISIS plans for switching many of Britain's factories to top-priority export production are being urgently studied by the Government.

At the same time, senior Ministers are making a "strict review" of the whole range of Government spending—including overseas military bases.

Mr. James Callaghan, Chancellor of the Exchequer, outlined the Government's new proposals in a statement to the Commons yesterday.

He said that these and other measures already announced would enable Britain to pay her way again in the world.

The Chancellor said that the £1,071,000,000 support for the £ from foreign bankers would give time to press forward with longer-term plans to strengthen the economy.

Priority

Mr. Callaghan went on: "The Government intend that we should be seen to be paying our way overseas as well as at home."

Priority, he said, was being given to "increasing our exports through measures that are being urgently worked out."

These will be in addition to the export rebate scheme.

Continued on Back Page

STERLING RISES TO NEW 'HIGH'

By ROBERT HEAD

THE £ hit its highest level for four months in world money markets yesterday, boosted by the £1,071,000,000 backing promised by thirteen international banks.

It rose by half a cent to 2 dollars 79¼ cents.

The fact that the £ has not yet crossed the official "par" rate of 2.80 dollars is a warning that foreign backing is no magic cure for the economic crisis.

It merely gives Britain time to tackle trade problems without having to worry about devaluation rumours.

City Column—Page 19. Battle of the £—Page 26.

Front page of the Daily Mirror on 27th November, two days after Brown's body was discovered. Frances Brown was twenty-one when she was murdered not twenty-three as stated in the Daily Mirror. © Mirrorpix.

Chapter 7

Murder at Kensington

On Wednesday 25th November 1964 (sorry Ron, nice try though), the naked body of prostitute Frances Brown aged twenty-one of 16a, Southerton Road, Hammersmith, was found on a rubbish heap on waste ground at the rear of a car park in Hornton Street, Kensington, London.

Photograph of Southerton Road Hammersmith early 1970s courtesy of Hammersmith and Fulham Archives and Local History Centre.

She was discovered near the Kensington Council Civil Defence training ground and control centre. Fellow prostitute Kim Taylor had last seen her alive on Friday 23rd October 1964. Taylor told the police that she and Brown had been soliciting together in Portobello Road and that they had both picked up clients in separate cars; the plan being that both vehicles would head in convoy to Chiswick Green. Brown and her client never arrived.

Now missing for just over a month, her badly decomposed body was found covered with branches, foliage and other debris.

A significant clue linking her killing to that of previous victims was that a number of her teeth were missing. Kensington police station was chosen as the murder hunt headquarters. A fifty strong murder squad concentrated their investigations in the Hammersmith, Notting Hill and Shepherds Bush districts.

Brown was last seen wearing a green two-piece suit with a dark fur collar, a plain white linen blouse, a blue and white check petticoat, blue brassière, black and pink panties, dark stockings and black suede shoes. She also carried black gloves and a light blue handbag. She was found stripped naked and none of her clothes, jewellery, or handbag were ever recovered.

At the Hammersmith inquest into the death of Frances Brown on Monday 30th November, pathologist Dr Donald Teare told the west London coroner Dr Gavin Thurston: *'I cannot give the cause of death yet. I think there is every reason why she should not be buried.'* Detective Superintendent William Marchant, who had also been in charge of the Mary Fleming murder inquiry, told the coroner that there was still some doubt about the victim's name as she had gone under the names of Frances Brown and Margaret McGowan. (McGowan was her mother's maiden name.) He said she had also used other aliases and had convictions for prostitution in London and Glasgow. (Brown had used a variety of aliases including Frances Quinn, Anne Sutherland and Susan Edwards.) Mr David Sutton the assistant Civil Defence Officer for Kensington told the coroner that he had seen a dustbin lid on waste ground at the rear of the Hornton Street car park.

Hornton Street car park Kensington. This area is now the location of the Kensington and Chelsea Borough Council Offices. The cost of reproducing this Mirrorpix photograph sponsored by David Webley, Abertillery.

He said he recognised it as belonging to a bin at his headquarters. He picked up the lid and saw the dead woman's head. The inquest was then adjourned until Wednesday 24th February 1965. On Wednesday 2nd December 1964 the police issued an appeal regarding the two men that had set off from Portobello Road in separate cars with Kim Taylor and Brown on the night Brown was last seen alive. They revealed new information at a press conference at Kensington police station, which was attended by Detective Chief Superintendent Jack Mannings and Detective Superintendent William Marchant.

Detective Superintendent William Marchant. Artwork by Tomas Jones, Brynmawr Foundation School. © 2011, Tomas Jones.

Marchant outlined events that led up to Brown's disappearance. He said: *'Brown was in the Warwick Castle public house Notting Hill on Friday the 23rd October with a twenty-one-year-old girlfriend [Kim Taylor] whose identity is being kept secret by the murder squad. [Brown and Taylor had repeatedly teased one another that evening in the Warwick Castle about the possibility of being the next "Stripper" victim.] The girls left the public house at 11.00pm and saw two men who knew each other, in separate cars at the junction of Westbourne Park Road and Portobello Road. The two prostitutes went across to the cars and chatted to the men. Then all four went into nearby Hayden Place and after a short discussion decided to go to Chiswick on "business." The cars with a girl in each then drove in the direction of Shepherds Bush but lost contact on the way. Brown's girlfriend, after finishing with her "client" then went to a jazz club in Ledbury Road, Notting Hill. The girls had a standing arrangement to meet at the club should they accidentally get separated, but on this occasion, Brown who was known by the surname of Quinn, to her friend did not show up.'*

Marchant then gave lengthy descriptions of both men and of the vehicles that they had been driving. He concluded by emphasising: *'It is possible that the men do not know that the girl in their company was later murdered. The police want anyone who can help identify the men to contact the murder squad at Kensington police station (WES 1113) or their local police.'* As Marchant acknowledged, the men could possibly have been oblivious to the murder. Or maybe they did know, but were married and terrified at the thought of having been rumbled for dabbling outside the marriage. Or they may have been involved in the murder. Whatever the case they never came forward or were ever identified. The inquest into the death of Frances Brown resumed at Hammersmith on Wednesday 24th February 1965. Brown's girlfriend Kim Taylor a factory machinist, gave the court her version of events that had occurred on the night of Brown's disappearance. She said: *'On 23rd October we began drinking in the afternoon and went right through until 11 o'clock in the evening. Frances consumed about eight whiskies and coke in the afternoon and had about eleven tots of whisky in the evening. We were picked up about 11 o'clock by two men in separate cars and that was the last time I saw her alive.'* Taylor told the coroner Dr Gavin Thurston, that although it was obvious Frances had been drinking she had not been *"slurring"* or *"blurring."*

After giving evidence of how he had found the body, Dennis John Sutton, Assistant Civil Defence Officer at Kensington, said that he was aware that a number of people parked their cars in the Hornton Street car park for the night. He concluded by stating that the area where he found the body was reasonably well concealed and at night was poorly lit. Pathologist Dr Donald Teare, told the inquest that he had visited the Hornton Street car park to examine the body of the deceased. He said: *'A post-mortem examination revealed that the cause of death was asphyxia due to pressure on the neck, which could not have been self-applied.'* On the recommendation of the coroner, the jury returned a verdict that *'a person or persons unknown'* had murdered Frances Brown.

Shortly before the inquest, on behalf of the police, Shaw Taylor made an appeal on the ATV television programme *'Police 5'* which resulted in a flood of information reaching the murder squad which by then had transferred from Kensington police station to Shepherds Bush. Every lead was checked that stemmed from that broadcast. Further to the *"Police 5"* appeal another police statement was issued regarding the man that was last seen with Brown on the night she vanished. The statement read: *'It is of importance that we interview this man as we believe he has information that is vital to our inquiries into the nude murders. The police are willing to meet this man anywhere, at any time, even through a third person. His confidence will be respected and his identity will not be disclosed.'* The pledge was given because the police believed that the man whom they wished to question may have been too embarrassed by his association with street girls to come forward.

Frances Brown was laid to rest in a paupers' grave, in plot JD 160 at Gunnersbury Cemetery, Gunnersbury Avenue, London W3 on Monday 15th March 1965.

Sixteen months prior to the discovery of her body, Brown had been a defence witness at the vice trial of fifty-year-old Dr Stephen Ward which began at the Old Bailey on 22nd July 1963. Ward had been a fashionable osteopath who had had many influential people including Sir Winston Churchill, Elizabeth Taylor and oil millionaire Jean Paul Getty as patients. As a portrait artist he had numerous members of the Royal Family sit for him, including Prince Philip, Lord Snowdon and the Duke and Duchess of Kent. Now he was reduced to being prosecuted for living off the immoral earnings of prostitution at his former flat at Wimpole Mews, Marylebone. Lurid details of his relationship with

Christine Keeler and her friend Mandy Rice-Davies were aired worldwide.

Ward, then of Bryanston Mews, Marylebone was charged: *'That he, being a man, did on diverse dates between January 1961 and 8th June 1963, knowingly live wholly or in part on the earnings of prostitution… contrary to… the Sexual Offences Act 1956.'* Ward had previously been a key figure in the 1961 Profumo Affair, a scandal that in 1963 rocked the ruling Conservative Party government led by Harold Macmillan. Cabinet Minister and MP John Profumo eventually resigned over his earlier tryst with nineteen-year-old showgirl and prostitute Christine Keeler. It had been alleged that Keeler may also have been having sexual relations with Yevgeny Ivanov, a naval attaché at the embassy of the Soviet Union, which attracted the concern of MI5. Ward later fared even worse. He took an overdose the night before the final day of his vice trial and was in a coma when the jury reached a guilty verdict. He died on Saturday 3rd August 1963 from the effects of a barbiturates overdose. Frances Brown had visited Ward at St Stephen's Hospital in Fulham while he lay in a coma. She had taken him flowers but was not allowed to see him.

Shaw Taylor MBE, 1924 – present. (2011) Shaw presented "Police 5" for thirty years, from 1962-1992, his catchphrase being "Keep 'em peeled!" Shaw's own production company also launched the highly successful crime fighting organisation "Crimestoppers." "Police 5" was directly responsible for the recovery of twelve priceless medallions stolen from Kew Palace in 1986. They were sent to Shaw anonymously after he had said on the programme "…the loser, a very distinguished lady, [the Queen] was not amused."

One good deed deserves another and in 1987 Shaw was awarded his MBE. At Buckingham Palace the Queen personally thanked Shaw for the return of the medallions and stated: "I think I owe you this one," to which he quipped: "You owe me twelve." Shaw, in his career has also been a Royal Commentator, Foreign Correspondent and Disk Jockey. He was the first DJ to interview The Beatles.

In 2008, aged eighty-three, Shaw featured as himself hosting "Police 5" in an episode of the BBC TV drama "Ashes to Ashes" set in October 1981.

Photograph courtesy of Clare Clifford and by kind permission of Shaw Taylor.

On Wednesday the 22nd April 2009, the author received an unexpected telephone call from forty-four-year-old Frank Quinn, the youngest child of Frances Brown. He related some important information about himself and his parents. Frank was born to Brown and her Dublin-born boyfriend Paul Quinn on 6th May 1964 in Lennoxtown, East Dunbartonshire, ten miles from Glasgow. Shortly after Frank's birth, Brown, with Quinn and the baby, moved in with her parents, fifty-year-old Francis and forty-four-year-old Helen Brown at 503, Gallowgate, one of the oldest thoroughfares in Glasgow.

A few weeks later all three then moved to Main Street, Bridgeton, Glasgow. In August 1964 the family then moved to 16a, Southerton Road, Hammersmith. Part of a letter that Frances sent to her parents in Scotland the month before she disappeared read: *'Well here I am writing to let you know that Paul and I have a great flat, one kitchen, one living room, one bedroom, one big lobby and it has a back garden and front…. Oh, mammy we have a television and hope to get a radiogram this week.'*

Sketch of Frances Brown and baby Frank based on a damaged photograph provided by Frank Quinn. Artwork by Aran Brown, Abertillery Comprehensive School. © 2011, Aran Brown.

Paul Quinn (also known as Pepe), 1936 – 2002. After the murder of his girlfriend, Quinn gave up his job and spent each day talking to prostitutes in a bid to track down her killer. He is seen here talking to a street girl in Shepherds Bush. Quinn died in Maidstone, Kent, from throat cancer. The cost of reproducing this Mirrorpix photograph sponsored by Blaenau Gwent County Borough Council and UK Steel Enterprise Limited.

The letter was signed Frances and Paul and included twenty-six kisses from four month old *'Frankie Junior.'* Later Brown's parents received a colour postcard of Piccadilly

Circus, which was posted via recorded delivery in Hammersmith on 1st October 1964. On it was written: *'Dear Mom, I received your letter ok. Paul myself and Baby doing fine and I hope all is the same at home. Lots of love Frances.'*

Francis and Helen Brown. Artwork by Michelle Homer, Tonypandy, Rhonda. © 2011, Michelle Homer. Artwork based on faded photographs supplied by Frank Quinn.

After being told of her daughter's murder Helen Brown told the police that when she first saw the writing on the postcard she had been concerned that it was not her daughter's. She said: *'I'm certain the message wasn't written by Frances, the handwriting was nothing like hers. When Frances writes to me she addresses it to Glasgow not Scotland and this card has Scotland on it.'* She also said that her daughter had never called her "Mom." She either called her *"Ma"* or *"Mammy."* She said: *'It had me worried for a while. But I convinced myself that I was fretting for nothing.'* Brown's maternal grandmother, Euphemia McGowan aged sixty-four of Abercrombie Street, Calton, Glasgow told the police: *'Frances and a man [Paul Quinn] lived in a house in [Main Street] Bridgeton for a few weeks earlier this year. The man was working as a scaffold erector but in August they went to London to live.'*

When Brown had failed to return to the flat at Southerton Road on 23rd October 1964, Paul Quinn set out to find her and eventually with baby Frank in arms, reported her missing to the Hammersmith police. He told them untruthfully that Frank wasn't his child, although he had brought him up as his own. He told the police that owing to work commitments he could no longer care for him. He was advised to take the baby to the local welfare office where arrangements were made for foster parents to take care of him. Quinn then went to Maidstone where he worked on a building site. While in a pub on Friday 27th November the landlord showed him the front page of that day's Daily Express. Quinn almost fainted when he saw the familiar face of the victim – his girlfriend Frances Brown. Quinn returned to Hammersmith to help the police with their inquiries.

Baby Frank was well cared for by Frederick and Alice Clara Scannell somewhere near Heathrow Airport (possibly, Bushey, Hertfordshire). At four years of age he went to St Etheldreda's Children's Home, Bedford and from the age of ten to sixteen he went to Alderwasley Hall Boarding School near Belper, Derbyshire. He visited his foster parents on a regular basis and it was during one of these visits, when he was aged fourteen that he begged Alice to tell him the truth about his real mother, which she did. At sixteen years of age Frank returned to his widowed foster mother who was by then living on the south coast in Dorset. He stayed with her until she died. He was then twenty-five. (Frederick died in 1979 aged sixty and Alice died in 1989 aged seventy-two.) In 1984 Frank met his elder sister Helen who had been born to Frances Brown in April 1961. Helen had been brought up by her grandparents Francis and Helen Brown in Scotland.

Following the author's appeal to readers of the Downs Mail, a Maidstone newspaper regarding information about Frank's father Paul Quinn, a daughter of Paul's phoned on 2nd September 2009 and gave some heartrending information. Carolina Quinn (Caz) aged twenty-one, Frank's half sister said that she and her sister Sarah aged thirty were aware of Frank's existence but had no idea of his whereabouts.

Their father had often broken down crying to them owing to the fact that he had abandoned Frank after Frances Brown's murder. From 1966 onwards, Paul Quinn made desperate attempts to regain custody of two-year-old Frank but the Hammersmith authorities fought tooth and nail to thwart his attempts. Frank is very bitter that the same authorities refused to give him any information about Paul Quinn. From the age of seventeen he had tried all avenues to contact his father. It's ironic that the authorities knew that both father and son were anxious to make contact yet did all they could to keep them apart. Until September 2009, Frank was unaware that his father had died in 2002. He was given Carolina's phone number and she and Sarah were overjoyed to speak with their half brother. Frank was shocked and delighted to learn about Carolina and Sarah, as he had no idea of their existence.

All three were united in Maidstone on Friday 25th September 2009. A very happy Marie Quinn, Carolina and Sarah's mother said she always knew in her heart that Frank would one day turn up on her doorstep. She said: *"For the first time in his life he is going to have a family album – at the age of forty five! I am just so pleased for my daughters that they have finally met him."* The November 2009 issue of the Downs Mail provided a double page feature on the Quinns' family reunion.

Frank Quinn 1964-present, (2011) pictured here with his sisters. Photograph courtesy of Downs Mail.

Frank's father, Paul Quinn had married Maureen Barclay in Maidstone in 1961 but the marriage soon soured and Maureen inadvertently introduced her husband to Frances Brown in 1962. That led to the end of the Quinns' marriage. After Frances Brown's murder, Paul Quinn settled in Maidstone where he married twenty-five-year-old Marie Oliver in 1975. That happy marriage produced Carolina and Sarah.

Left to right. Carolina, Marie and Sarah Quinn, with Sarah holding Carolina's 2½-year-old son Lenny. Marie is holding a photograph of her late husband, Paul Quinn. Photograph courtesy of Peter Erlam, Downs Mail.

Frank is also aware that he has an elder brother, Paul Anthony Quinn whom Brown had given birth to at Queen Charlotte's Hospital Hammersmith, in March 1963. Shortly after the birth, Frances Brown suffered a nervous breakdown and moved to Smethwick near Birmingham, to recover. She, Paul Quinn and baby Paul stayed with Quinn's former mother-in-law with whom Quinn was still on very good terms.

Brown was in Smethwick when she learned from newspaper reports that her former friend, prostitute Vickie Barrett had given evidence against Dr Stephen Ward at his vice trial at the Old Bailey. Brown had in her possession a number of sketches of herself that were drawn by Stephen Ward at her former address in Shepherds Bush. She was extremely proud that Ward, a man with many influential friends, had taken a kindly interest in her. Brown told Quinn that she was going to London to speak in defence of Ward, which led to a blazing row. She went back to London regardless, with Quinn and Paul Anthony was taken into care in Smethwick.

Vickie Barrett (real name Janet Barker) had told the Old Bailey jury at Dr Stephen Ward's trial that she had performed sexual acts at Ward's flat up to as many as three times a week. Ward, she said, had provided the wealthy clients and that the biggest share of the proceeds went into his pockets. 4th nudes' victim Irene Lockwood and 5th victim Helene Barthelemy had both known a number of the women named in the Ward court case. Barthelemy had previously been involved in a photo-blackmail racket with prostitute Veronica Walsh aged twenty-two. Ironically, in a completely different case Walsh was killed by Colin Welt Fisher aged thirty-three. Fisher, an engineer who had admitted that he and Walsh had been high on drugs prior to the killing was jailed for life at the Old Bailey on 2nd July 1963 for Walsh's murder. Irene Lockwood had given evidence against Fisher during his trial. *Twists and turns!*

Frances Brown entered the Old Bailey dock during Dr Stephen Ward's trial and received her first taste of fame amidst celebrities and celebrity spotters. She told the Old Bailey jury that she and Vickie Barrett had been friends and had solicited together but had only visited Ward's flat on two occasions. The first time was when Ward had taken a personal fancy to Barrett and the second when all three had just enjoyed a social evening. She refuted Barrett's claim that Ward had been a pimp or had in any way lived off immoral earnings. Throughout the hearing, journalist, broadcaster and author, Ludovic Kennedy heard evidence from both sides. Regarding Brown he observed; *'a small bird-like woman with a pale face and a fringe, who teetered down the court and into the witness box.'* He noted how Brown had been quite definite in her answers in response to questions put to her. The things she said had a ring of truth to them, which is normal when a person is telling the truth. Kennedy concluded in his 1964 book *"The Trial of Stephen Ward"* that the guilty verdict handed down on Ward had been a total miscarriage of justice. On page 241 of his book, which was reprinted in 1991 by A New Portway Book published by Chivers Press Bath, Kennedy quotes from a letter that Ward had written to Vickie Barrett shortly before his suicide. It read: *'I don't know what it was or who it was that made you do what you did. But if you have any decency left, you should tell the truth like Ronna Ricardo. [Margaret Ricardo, who had given evidence against Ward.] You owe this not to me, but to everyone who may be treated like you or like me in future.'*

About half an hour after Ward died, Daily Telegraph journalist Barry O'Brien who had been a witness for the defence at Ward's trial confronted Vickie Barrett at her lodgings at Clanricarde Gardens, Notting Hill, with a photocopy of Ward's letter to her. After O'Brien had put questions to Barrett about the truthfulness of her evidence against Ward, Barrett had broken down crying: *'It was all lies. But I never thought he would die. I didn't want him to die…. It was not all lies. I did go to the flat but it was only to do business with Stephen Ward. It was not true that I went with other men.'* O'Brien asked Barrett why she had lied in court and she said the reason she did so was because a police officer had warned her that if she didn't she would never again be allowed to solicit in Notting Hill and if she was caught she would go to prison for nine months or more. O'Brien offered to take Barrett to Ward's solicitor Mr Wheatley, to retract her earlier statement to the police. Barrett's landlady however persuaded her to keep her mouth shut and she then retracted her confession to O'Brien that she had told the court lies.

Police corruption! MI5! Retractions! Retracted retractions! Russian espionage! Did Brown's brief court appearance seal her fate? Was she murdered because of her link to the vice scandal? The day before his arrest for living off immoral earnings, Ward had appeared in a television documentary. He told Desmond Wilcox, the future husband of television producer Esther Rantzen, that when his connection to MP John Profumo had become apparent two years earlier, he had informed MI5 about Profumo's affair with Christine Keeler. MI5 denied that they had been told. Were MI5 behind Brown's murder as some have suggested? That just doesn't make sense.

There was no other apparent link between Brown's involvement in the Ward-Profumo affair and the previous five murdered prostitutes. (Rees to Fleming) Or was there? Author and broadcaster Anthony Summers once claimed that murdered prostitute Hannah Tailford was herself peripherally connected to the Profumo Affair. But that would still leave four murder victims with no connection to Profumo or Ward. Make that five!

Chapter 8

Murder at Acton

On Monday 11th January 1965 prostitute Bridget Esther O'Hara aged twenty-eight failed to return home to her flat at 41 Agate Road Hammersmith, London, after a night out.

Photograph of Agate Road Hammersmith early 1970s courtesy of Hammersmith and Fulham Archives and Local History Centre.

She'd gone missing before. No problem. She'll turn up soon. And she did. But there was a problem. She turned up five weeks later. Naked and dead! And with a number of teeth missing! She was found on Tuesday 16th February at about 11.00am by Leonard Beauchamp a twenty-six-year-old Polish electrical fitter from Northolt who worked at Surgical Equipment Supplies Limited on the Heron Trading Estate, Acton, west London. The crime scene area near Beauchamp's workplace was a strip of land between a chain link fence and a storage shed and had frequently been used by fly tippers. Beauchamp told the police that he had been rummaging amongst the debris for anything worth taking home. But, he unexpectedly found something the police wouldn't allow him to take. This piece of debris had to go to the mortuary to find the cause of her death.

Leonard Beauchamp pictured at the front of the storage shed. O'Hara's body was found at the rear of this building. The cost of reproducing this Mirrorpix photograph sponsored by Blaenau Gwent County Borough Council and UK Steel Enterprise Limited.

About two and a half hours after the discovery of O'Hara's body, pathologist Dr David Bowen and coroner Dr Harold Broadbridge arrived at the scene. They were led to a narrow strip of ground, which was located between a chain-link fence and the rear of the storage shed overlooking the Central Line running between North Acton and West Acton stations. After dried vegetation was removed from the body, Dr Bowen carried out a preliminary examination before ordering the body be taken to Acton mortuary where he carried out a post-mortem later that same day.

He noted that the victim was 5ft 2ins tall, of medium build, with dark hair and had a small nose. She had long eyelashes, arched eyebrows and light brown eyes. Both her ears were pierced and she had a tattoo of a heart on her left forearm. Inside the heart was the name *"Nick"* or *"Mick."* (It turned out that the name was Mick.) Dr Bowen concluded that the cause of death was asphyxia due to pressure on the face and neck.

Detective Superintendent William Baldock was initially appointed investigating officer and set up the murder headquarters at Brentford police station. He concentrated his efforts specifically around the Hammersmith district. (On 19th November 2010 the author contacted William Baldock at his home in North London. Then aged ninety-four he was the last surviving high ranking police officer involved in the Hammersmith nudes' murders inquiries. He said that he had his theories as to who the killer was but didn't want to get involved. He mused: *'I'm ninety-four now you know.' 'I hope you get your congratulations card off the Queen in six years time Mr Baldock.' 'Yes if she's still alive'*, he replied chuckling. William who is selling his house in Finchley *"to start a new life"* still drives his car and is well cared for by his neighbours who regularly check on him "to make sure he hasn't fallen off his perch.")

The police keeping guard at the rear of the shed where Bridget's body was found. The cost of reproducing this Getty Image photograph sponsored by Chat magazine.

Detective Superintendent William Baldock, 1916-present. (2011) Artwork by Tomas Jones, Brynmawr Foundation School. © 2011, Tomas Jones.

This photograph was taken from the railway bridge at Westfields Road, Acton. The large storage shed on the left is where Bridget's body was found between the rear of the shed and the fence. Inset is pathologist Dr David Bowen. Photograph courtesy of Gillian Kirk.

O'Hara's body was believed to have been kept for a number of weeks in some kind of storage shed and had partly mummified. It was also believed that the body had been removed from storage and dumped at the Heron Trading Estate shortly before it had been discovered. After the discovery, twenty-eight-year-old Thelma Schwartz née Cheesman of Mellitus Street, East Acton, who worked as a cleaner at the trading estate, gave the police some vital information. She said that at about 5.40am on the morning of Friday 12th February, four days before Beauchamp's discovery, she heard suspicious noises in the dark at the crime scene area. She had missed her lift that morning from her supervisor Mrs Tyson and had to walk the dark lonely route to work at Zonal Film Facilities Ltd. As she was crossing a bridge at Westfields Road, Acton, which led to the trading estate, she heard loud rustling noises coming from the rear of a shed which backed on to the railway embankment to her right.

Thelma Schwartz, 1937 – present. (2011)

The bridge at Westfields Road, Acton. Thelma had walked to work on the right side of the bridge. Just as she had passed the Bridge Café, which can be seen on the left she heard the rustling sound. As she approached the end of the bridge (near the coach) the rustling got louder. Just a few yards away to her right was where the killer was hiding the body of Bridget O'Hara.

Terrified, Thelma ran on tiptoe to work. In two minds as to whether the rustling came from an animal or a person she kept quiet about what she had heard until the body of O'Hara was found four days later. Thelma, who was seventy-three in 2011 realises how fortunate she is to be alive today. If the killer had twigged that she had heard him he would surely have done his best to silence her. Just three weeks after her experience she finished at Zonal, terrified that the killer may lie in wait for her in one of the many unlit doorways of the trading estate. Thelma and her husband Kenneth often talked about her potential near miss. Kenneth, who Thelma married in 1953, died in November 2006. Thelma now lives at Braybrook Street, East Acton. (Braybrook Street was the scene of the murders of three police officers on August 12th 1966. Harry Roberts, John Duddy and John Witney were convicted and jailed for the murders of DS Christopher Head, DC David Wombwell and PC Geoffrey Fox. Duddy died in prison in 1981, Witney was released in 1991 and was beaten to death at his home in Bristol eight years later. Roberts in 2011 was awaiting parole after serving forty five years in prison.)

The police were sure that Thelma had heard the killer in the dark, covering Bridget's body with leaves and other dead vegetation and that she herself had had a close encounter with the killer. What the forensic laboratory officers found on O'Hara's naked body convinced the police that they were getting closer to apprehending the killer. As with the three previous victims, O'Hara's body yielded minute traces of dust and paint particles.

Soon after the discovery of the body, Detective Chief Inspector John du Rose of New Scotland Yard was put in overall charge of the murder inquiry and had well over three hundred uniformed and CID officers and three hundred Special Patrol Group members at his disposal. Known for his ability to solve murders in less than four days, he acquired the nickname *"Four Day Johnny."* He had the dubious honour at that time of conducting the largest criminal manhunt in British history.

Within two days of the discovery of the body of O'Hara it seemed as if *"Four Day Johnny"* had cracked the case when, on Thursday 18th February, thirty-three-year-old Wimpey Autos proprietor William Edward Chissell was questioned by John du Rose about her death. If he was the killer then all six definite nudes' murders (Tailford to O'Hara) would most likely be laid at his doorstep. Officers from Scotland Yard's forensic laboratory descended on Chissell's panel beating and cellulose paint-spraying garage at 1a, Barb Mews, Hammersmith.

Chissell's garage at Hammersmith.

They took away specimens of oil, grease, iron filings and dried paint. Excitement amongst the police was raised when pieces of cloth found in the garage turned out to be remnants of women's clothing. Chissell, whom the police suspected was involved in the murders was held and questioned but was arrested for a different offence. He was charged with possessing a gun and ammunition without a firearms certificate.

He denied all knowledge of the gun, which was found in his garage. He believed (or at least he said he believed) it had been hidden in his garage without his knowledge or had been planted by the police as a means of securing an arrest to question him about the nudes' murders. Local and national newspapers covered the arrest of Chissell on the gun charge and, a nod being as good as a wink, led to many thinking that the nudes' murder inquiry was soon going to be over. Chissell who had been held from 18th to 26th February was eventually released from custody and all charges were dropped. Unfortunately mud sticks and there are still people today who will name Chissell as the nudes' murderer.

Disappointed by this development but undeterred, John du Rose who was absolutely convinced that the bodies of some of the murder victims had been stored in or near a paint-spraying workshop made a sweep of a twenty-four square mile area of west London to find the location.

The Bridge Café at Westfields Road, Acton, which is just yards away from where the body of Bridget O'Hara was found, was at the height of the investigation, swarming with police. For weeks the café's owners, Frank Marcangelo and his brother Gerry were grilled, as were scores of their customers who included henchmen of the Kray twins. Gerry remembers well the impact that finding O'Hara's body had on Leonard Beauchamp. He said: *'I remember it like yesterday. A little fellow he was. He was never the same again.'*

The Marcangelo brothers and the Bridge Café again shot into the limelight (in 2009) when filming of Sir Alan Sugar's, *"The Apprentice"* took place at the premises. The contestants met at the café for debriefing before Sir Alan's famous, *'You're fired'* tirade at the unsuccessful wannabes.

'The Daily Star Sunday' of 17th May 2009 did a full-page feature about the café entitled: *"Serial Killer Link to Apprentice Café."* Frank aged sixty-four and Gerry aged sixty-seven (in 2011) still run the café, which their father had opened in 1962. (The Marcangelo brothers are not related to the designer of fresco paintings in the Sistine Chapel at the Vatican!)

Just a short walk away from the café was the former factory known as Ultra Electric Limited, a firm that produced affordable radios that were advertised extensively by comedian Arthur Askey. Ultra had relocated from Chalk Farm to the Heron Trading Estate in 1935. Two of the 1,600 employees were Muriel Amelia Eady and John Christie. Christie for four years was also a War Reserve Constable at Harrow Road police station. In October 1944 Christie invited Muriel to his house at Notting Hill with the promise that he had a cure for her chronic catarrh. He told Muriel that he had invented a special inhaler. Into a jar he put some inhalant disguised with the odour of Friar's Balsam. He had made two holes in the top of the jar, in one of which he inserted a small hose that he ran to the gas supply. The tube ran into the liquid in the bottom of the jar and another tube, not in the liquid came out of the other hole, which was designed to stop the concoction from smelling like gas. Christie invited Muriel to inhale the concoction and within one minute she was unconscious. He then strangled and killed her.

Justice eventually caught up with John Reginald Halliday Christie of 10 Rillington Place, Notting Hill, when he was hanged on 15th July 1953. He had been charged with, and found guilty of the murder of his wife Ethel in 1952. It transpired that he had also murdered twenty-one-year-old Ruth Fuerst in 1943; the earlier mentioned Muriel Eady aged thirty-one in 1944, and *two prostitutes* in 1953; Rita Nelson aged twenty-five and Kathleen Maloney aged twenty-six. The same year he also murdered Hectorina MacLennan also aged twenty-six. It is now believed by some that Christie also murdered twenty-year-old Beryl Evans and her thirteen-month-old baby Geraldine in November 1949. Beryl's husband, twenty-five-year-old Timothy Evans also of 10 Rillington Place, was hanged on 9th March 1950 after being wrongly convicted of the murder of his baby daughter Geraldine.

The inquest into the death of Bridget O'Hara was opened at Ealing on Friday 19th February 1965. Bridget's brothers, William and Matthew Moore who lived in London and Christopher, who had travelled from Dublin, attended the inquest. Their mother Mary Moore aged fifty-two who had also flown in was too distraught to face up to the ordeal and stayed away. (Coach and taxi driver Charlie Cheesman, the father of Thelma Schwartz, the cleaner at the Heron Trading Estate, was sent to pick up Christopher and Mary from Heathrow Airport. From there they were whisked to Shepherds Bush police station, the murder inquiry headquarters having been moved from Brentford.) The husband of the deceased, Michael Joseph O'Hara, a scaffolder of 41 Agate Road, Hammersmith, gave evidence of identification. The coroner, Dr Harold Broadbridge told O'Hara: *'I am still making inquiries into your wife's death. The funeral will have to stand in abeyance. As soon as it is possible for the inquest to take place my officer will let you know.'* After the pathologist Dr David Bowen said that the death was caused by pressure on the neck leading to asphyxia, the hearing was adjourned until 17th March 1965 after which it was again adjourned until 9th February 1966.

On Friday 26th February 1965 a young woman the same size, and with similar looks to Bridget O'Hara was paraded by the police around the yard at Shepherds Bush police station in front of dozens of newspaper photographers and television cameras. She was dressed in clothes identical to the ones O'Hara had worn when she was last seen alive on 11th January. They were hoping that someone, after seeing the pictures on television or in the papers, would have their memory jogged. O'Hara's description was given as follows: *"Bridie is described as 5ft 2ins tall with short brunette hair. She wore a long grey and white herringbone coat with a matching scarf with a matching fringe. On her feet she wore calf-length, high-heeled, black leather boots. She may have worn dark rimmed spectacles."* Unfortunately the appeal produced nothing to help in the investigation.

A policeman involved in the Bridget O'Hara murder inquiry spotted this woman in the street. Noticing the striking resemblance between her and O'Hara he invited her to pose as the victim. The cost of reproducing this Getty Image photograph sponsored by Chat magazine.

Just as the police believed that they had come to the end of the line in their fruitless search for a lead, they came up with a pattern that they had so desperately been seeking. The search ended near the spot where the body of the last victim Bridget O'Hara was found. The police were now absolutely convinced that the body had been stored not far from where it had been discovered. And it had been. The storage place was a building used to house an electricity transformer at the vacant premises of Napier Aero Engines at Mansfield Road, Heron Trading Estate.

Detective Chief Superintendent John Valentine Ralph du Rose pointing to the transformer building at the Heron Trading Estate, Acton, where at least four of the victims were stored sometimes for weeks before being dumped in various parts of west London. This building was approximately 150 yards away from the rear of the shed where O'Hara's body had been found and has since been demolished.

John du Rose was a descendant of a family of Huguenots who fled to Britain from France at the time of the Duke of Alva's persecution in 1569. He was born in London in 1911 and started his police career in 1931. The following year he married Constance Chapman, who died in 1968. In 1970, fifty-nine year-old du Rose then married thirty-six-year-old WPC Merle Taylor. Merle had acted as a decoy prostitute in the early part of 1965 in the hope of drawing out the killer. Du Rose served thirty-nine years with the London Metropolitan Police, before retiring in 1970. He died in Great Yarmouth in 1980. The cost of reproducing this Mirrorpix photograph sponsored by Cwmtillery Communities First, Abertillery.

Workers at a number of factories used the empty but unsecured Napier Aero Engines premises (see front cover) as a short cut to reach the Bridge Café in Westfields Road. They would have walked to within yards of the rear of the storage shed where Bridget's body was hidden. About 150 yards away from the shed was the transformer building and it faced a paint-spraying shop. The shop belonged to Shaw and Kilburn, a firm of motor engineers and coachbuilders, a company co-founded by entrepreneur and sportsman Drysdale Kilburn, a descendant of south Wales ironmaster Crawshay Bailey. Access to the transformer building was available via large double doors held in place by sliding bolts thus making it easy for anyone to enter.

Laboratory tests proved without a shadow of a doubt that dust and paint particles found on O'Hara's body and in her hair produced an identical pattern to that found in the transformer building. Particles of paint from the paint shop had entered the transformer building through a six-foot by three-foot wire mesh ventilation window that faced the paint-spraying shop. Also soot and dust particles from chimneys near the transformer building were identical to that found on the last four victims.

The police were now sure that it was only a matter of time before the killer would be identified. They knew that he had an intimate knowledge of the estate and possibly worked there. The main problem though was that there were 7,214 personnel and visitors to the estate, current and past to interview. Du Rose adopted a strategy that he hoped would spook the killer. He made numerous newspaper, television and radio appeals, not just to the public but also to the killer himself. It would be highly improbable that the killer would wish to avoid reading the newspapers or watching the television news and he would be sure of what steps the police were taking to apprehend him and stop the slaughter.

Du Rose organised a steady stream of propaganda statements to the press including ones such as: *'We have whittled the number of suspects down to twenty.'* As time passed he played a masterstroke by claiming that the number of suspects was reduced to three and then finally made the statement that the police now knew who the killer was.

Sir Ranulph Robert Maunsell Bacon QPM, 1906-1988. Chief Constable of Devon 1947-1961. Assistant Commissioner "A" London Metropolitan Police 1961-1963. Assistant Commissioner "C" London Metropolitan Police 1963-1966. Knighted in 1966. Photograph courtesy of Heritage and Learning Resource, Devon and Cornwall Constabulary. The cost of reproducing this photograph sponsored by Shirley Mainwaring, Cwmtillery.

On Wednesday 17th March 1965 Scotland Yard's Assistant Commissioner Ranulph

Bacon made a television appeal to anyone who had information about the killer. He said: *'It may be because of your affection for this person or because of a misconceived loyalty that you hesitate, but the means of bringing to notice the identity of the person concerned lies within your power. I expect you must be a very worried person. Should you fail to carry out this very public and moral duty there could rest on your conscience the possible death of yet another young woman.'*

Fortunately, Bridget was the last of the nudes' murder victims. She was laid to rest at Hammersmith (New) Cemetery, Mortlake, on Wednesday 16th June 1965 in plot number C19 406. Her grave is just a short distance away from the spot where the body of Gwynneth Rees had been discovered two years earlier in a makeshift grave at the rubbish tip.

Bridget's grave is still well cared for.

The formal inquest into the death of Bridget O'Hara was concluded at Hammersmith Coroner's Court on Wednesday 9th February 1966, some thirteen months after she had disappeared. Dr Harold Broadbridge, having retired as coroner at the end of March 1965, took the unusual step of coming out of retirement to conclude the inquest he had opened and adjourned twelve months earlier, thus preserving continuity. O'Hara's inquest was the fifth of the eight murdered prostitutes over which he had presided.

Michael Joseph O'Hara told the inquest that he and his wife had married in Dublin in 1962. In January 1965 they had parted, but on the day of Bridget's disappearance they had got together at their flat at Agate Road, Hammersmith. At 9.30pm the same evening Bridget had told him that she was going to visit a friend at Brook Green.

A police officer told the inquest that he had made enquiries and found that Bridget hadn't gone to visit her friend but had been last seen leaving the Shepherds Bush Hotel on Shepherds Bush Green with a man at closing time.

After a steady stream of witnesses gave their evidence, the foreman of the all-male jury of eight contributed the final words. After conferring with his fellow jurors for less than half a minute, he stated that the jury had unanimously decided that *'a person or persons unknown'* had murdered Bridget.

Dr Broadbridge's retirement party in March 1965. He is seen here with his coroner's officers and pathologists.
Rear row left to right: AGR Ackland Snow – J Tidy – EC Mortimore – A Bridges – J Little.
Front Row left to right: Bernard Fox – Dr Donald Teare – Dr Harold George Broadbridge –?Killpack – Dr David
Bowen. Dr Broadbridge was appointed President of the Coroners' Society of England and Wales in 1962. At
the Annual Dinner of the Society held that year at the Connaught Rooms, Covent Garden, he must have been
very highly regarded to have been able to invite and receive such eminent guests as Lord Justice Diplock, Lord
Evans, Sir Joseph Simpson, (Commissioner of the Metropolitan Police) and Sir Theobald Matthew, (Director
of Public Prosecutions.) Photograph courtesy of Dr Broadbridge's daughter Gillian Kirk.

Regarding John du Rose's earlier statement about knowing who the killer was, whether he knew or not, a fruitful arrest was never made. The killings stopped and the police task force set up to catch the killer was reduced and finally disbanded. DCI John du Rose who had started his career in the police force in 1931 retired from the Metropolitan Police in 1970. By that time he had attained the rank of Deputy Assistant Commissioner at New Scotland Yard.

On 2nd April 1970, two days after his retirement du Rose was interviewed on the BBC current affairs programme *"24 Hours"* by presenter and top selling author Tom Mangold. He told Mangold: '*As time went on, of course, we realised that the suspect, whoever he was, must be reading the news of what was going on, the activities of the police and so on. And so we got the press and the radio and the television on our side, and we fed them stories every day. This was our way of communication with the murderer and we hoped by this means to start him up, to get him frightened, to make him run, to do something, which would point the finger towards his guilt. And I think eventually he became so frightened he took his own life. And this was within a matter of weeks of this inquiry starting by me in February 1965.*'

He also said that the unnamed person who had committed suicide had already been a suspect at the time of his death. He said: '*Now we couldn't talk to him, he was dead. We could only ask questions, check his activities, his movements, where he associated and so on. And when you bear in mind that there were six takings and six droppings of the body, we had twelve occasions on which to check an individual out. A wonderful set of circumstances really to pinpoint an individual. Not just one murder…but on twelve occasions this man could have been available to have committed all these murders. And even now I am not in a position to name this man. He has relatives who are still alive, it would reflect on them. It would be utterly wrong and we don't do that type of thing.'*

Bridget and Michael O'Hara on their wedding day. The cost of reproducing this Mirrorpix photograph sponsored by Blaenau Gwent County Borough Council and UK Steel Enterprise Limited.

Scotland Yard officially distanced themselves from du Rose's claims, asserting the case was still unsolved. This was in spite of the fact that in October 1965 a huge dossier on the case had been laid before the Metropolitan Police Commissioner. This included a statement that it was believed that the killer had indeed committed suicide.

In 1971 John du Rose wrote his autobiography entitled *"Murder Was My Business,"* which was published by WH Allen. Towards the end of chapter ten – *"Jack the Stripper,"* he made the statement *'We could never forget that no woman was safe until the killer was in our hands, but it was not to be and within a month of the murder of Bridie O'Hara, the man I wanted to arrest took his own life. Without a shadow of a doubt the weight of our investigation and the enquiries that we made about him led to the killer committing suicide. We had done all we possibly could but faced with his death, no positive evidence was available to prove or disprove our belief that he was in fact the man we had been seeking. Because he was never arrested, or stood trial, he must be considered innocent and will therefore never be named.'*

According to the Scotland Yard Serious Crime Review Group, who between November 2006 and May 2007 re-investigated the Hammersmith nudes' murders, du Rose's suspect whom; *"I wanted to arrest"* had indeed been a suspect in 1965.

He was a man who had had connections to the Heron Trading Estate, Acton, through his former employment as a night security patrolman. (He worked for a while with Night Security, Paradise Walk, Chelsea, now a defunct company.) He also had connections with prostitutes through a family member's employment as a brothel maid. (This person's name is known but will be withheld.) He did commit suicide shortly after the murder of Bridget O'Hara the last victim and the murders did then stop. However the official inquiry by the police in 1965 concluded that the suspect was in Scotland on the night of 11th January 1965 when Bridget O'Hara disappeared, and there was no evidence to connect him with any of the other prostitutes or to place him in a position where he had the opportunity to abduct them.

In 2006 author David Seabrook published his book *"Jack of Jumps"* which provided detailed information on all eight prostitutes who were murdered between 1959 and 1965. Regarding du Rose's suspect he states on page 353: 'Police found no evidence of any description to link this man to the murdered women, and the fact that he was in Scotland on 11th January, the date of O'Hara's disappearance, served to eliminate him from the inquiry. He *"will never be named"* because he was framed, his suicide exploited for fame and glory by

John du Rose.
John Valentine Ralph du Rose.
By any other name he'd stink as sweet.'

Seabrook names the man who *"will never be named"* as forty-five-year-old Mungo Ireland who resided at the time of his death at his four bedroom maisonette at 132 Tildesley Road, Putney, London.

Mungo Ireland lived in this block of maisonettes.

Amazingly, the police re-investigation in 2006-2007 resulted in a new conclusion about Ireland's possible involvement in the nudes' murders. Their conclusion was: *'The circumstantial evidence against Mungo Ireland is very strong and it was the view of the officers conducting the most recent review of this case (2006-2007) that he was most likely to be responsible.'* If Mungo Ireland was in Scotland on the night of the disappearance of Bridget O'Hara how could he have been involved in her disappearance and death? The only way he could have been involved was if someone else was working with him as part of a team! Or is there another explanation?

(A puzzling feature is that after John du Rose's retirement in 1970, he claimed he knew who the nudes' killer was prior to Ireland's suicide. He said that in 1965 he had told *"porkies"* to the press to draw the killer out which frightened him into taking his own life. If he truly knew that Ireland was the killer, why two months later in May 1965 would he have gone to all the trouble of interviewing over 7000 potential suspects who had had connections to the Heron Trading Estate?)

Following a request to New Scotland Yard regarding the Heron Trading Estate inquiry and whether Ireland had been a suspect in March 1965, the following reply was received on 16th July 2010. *'On 6th May 1965 enquiries were extended to include all personnel and visitors to the entire Heron Estate. This resulted in 7,214 current and past workers being interviewed. This would suggest he [John du Rose] didn't already know who the murderer was.'*

Very little is known about Mungo Ireland. His paternal grandparents from Dundee, Scotland, were Mungo Brodie Ireland (1855-1913) (a labourer) and Mary Jane Ireland née Fields (1863-1935). Mungo Brodie and Mary Jane married on 1st January 1883 in Dundee. They had a son, David Ireland (a calendar worker) who, while living at 31 Princes Street Dundee, married Annie Johnstone (a jute preparer) of 112 Cowgate, Dundee on 1st January 1904 at St Rogues Church, Dundee. David was twenty and Annie was nineteen. Annie gave birth to Mungo at 9.40am on Thursday 17th April 1919 at 48 Crescent Lane, Dundee.

David Ireland (circled) at a union meeting, time and place unknown, and Annie, left with either her sisters or sisters-in-law. Photographs supplied by David and Annie's granddaughter.

In the early hours of 18th October 1964 while working for Night Security, Paradise Walk, Chelsea, Mungo, in an intoxicated state was admitted to Middlesex Hospital with a superficial head injury. He told nurses that he had been patrolling near the Renault car factory at the Heron Trading Estate, Acton when two unknown persons set upon him.

(The factory has now been replaced by the Renault car sales dealership.) He continued to work for Night Security for just over a week and then handed in his notice.

On 13th November 1964 he accepted a job as a factory cleaner with New Century Group Limited in Harlesden, London. On 28th November, three days *after* the body of Frances Brown was discovered in Kensington he accepted the position of foreman cleaner at Jute Industries in Dundee.

He stayed with family members in Scotland while his wife and five children remained in Putney. On 11th February 1965, the day *before* O'Hara's body was dumped at the Heron Trading Estate, Ireland arrived back in London. Although Ireland's work records indicate that he was in Scotland on the night of the disappearance of Bridget O'Hara, Scotland Yard now believe it is possible that these may have been falsified and that it was at least feasable that he could have flown from Scotland to London on the night of Bridget's disappearance on 11th January, killed her, taken her to the Heron Trading Estate and left her body in the electricity sub-station before flying back to Scotland. He could then have sat tight in Scotland for four weeks before returning to London to move the dead body of Bridget to where it was found on 16th February.

On Tuesday 2nd March1965 Ireland had been watching television at his home at 132 Tildesley Road, Ashburton Estate, Putney. He fell asleep on the sofa and his wife Elizabeth whom he had married in Malta in the 1940s went to bed leaving him sleeping. At about midnight Elizabeth heard Mungo's vehicle, registration number YUL 333 drive off from outside their maisonette and she went back to sleep. The following morning she awoke and found a suicide note in her husband's handwriting.

It read: *'I can't stick it any longer. It may be my fault but not all of it. I'm sorry Harry is a burden to you. Give my love to the kid. [s?] Farewell. Jock. PS. To save you and the police looking for me I'll be in the garage.'* This referred to a lock-up garage a few hundred yards away at Solna Avenue, Putney.

Elizabeth sent her seventeen-year-old son David the 700 yards or so to see if Mungo was in the garage. When David returned he told his mother that his father appeared to be sleeping in the car. Elizabeth screamed at her twenty-two-year-old daughter Anna to go quickly to check if her father was alright. She returned shocked and ashen-faced. Elizabeth then raced to the premises where indeed she found her husband was dead. (Ireland had killed himself in his Ford Consul which he had bought new at the Earls Court Motor Show. He had often sat in the window of his maisonette at Tildesley Road admiring his pride and joy.)

An inquest was held into the death of Mungo Ireland on Tuesday 9th March 1965 at Battersea, London. Elizabeth Ireland told the inquest of events leading up to the discovery of her husband's body. PC Charles Siddall told the inquest that after being informed of the death of the deceased he went to the garage at Solna Avenue and saw Ireland lying across the front seat of his car with his head on the steering wheel. He said an ambulance arrived at the scene and the crew tried to revive him but without success. Siddall said: *'I found that the engine of the car was not running and the petrol gauge showed empty. I found that with the ignition on the engine would not start.'* It appeared that the car had run dry of fuel during the night while ticking over in the garage.

(On the morning that Ireland's body was found, he had been due to appear before Acton Magistrates' Court to face a charge of failing to stop his car after being involved in a road traffic accident.)

The coroner Dr Gavin Thurston remarked: *'It is significant that his death occurred on the morning he was due to answer a summons. There had been a change in his habits and general behaviour recently. He had been drinking rather heavily shortly before his death. The note to his wife clearly explained where he could be found and gave a clear indication of his intentions.'* Recording a verdict of suicide, Dr Thurston said Ireland had died from asphyxiation after inhaling car exhaust fumes.

Solna Avenue, West Putney, where Ireland committed suicide.

Did Ireland commit suicide to save facing Acton magistrates over a trifling motoring charge or did John du Rose push him over the edge with his press statements? Ireland was buried in plot 190, block 15 at Putney Vale Cemetery. (Another puzzling feature is that if Ireland had been a suspect before his suicide why was there no forensic evidence in his car, garage or home to link him to the killings, bearing in mind that he had killed himself only a short time after the last two murders?)

Who was the *"Harry"* referred to in Ireland's suicide note? Following a full year's research into the mystery, the answer was eventually provided with the help of the detective skills of *'Taggart'* creator Glenn Chandler and Abertillery computer whiz-kid, Jon Nixey. *"Harry"* was the younger brother of Mungo Ireland. His real name? – Henry Johnstone Ireland. Maltese born Elizabeth Ireland née Formosa had married Henry's brother Mungo during World War Two. Able seaman Mungo Ireland had been a sailor on HMS Penelope and had been mentioned in dispatches for his exceptional heroism having saved many of his fellow crew members lives in various wartime skirmishes. HMS Penelope was holed so many times by enemy bomb fragments that she acquired the nickname *"HMS Pepperpot."* On 18th February 1944, HMS Penelope was torpedoed twice within sixteen minutes by the German submarine U – 410. It sank with the loss of 415 men while 206 survived. (Could Mungo's wartime trauma have caused him to hit the bottle?) Mungo's grandson David Ireland possesses his five wartime medals. They include: The Star of Burma, The Star of Africa and The Star of Italy.

Mungo and Elizabeth's first child Anna was born in Malta in 1943. Elizabeth Ireland arrived at Liverpool on March 18th 1944 with ten-month-old Anna. They had travelled aboard the Canadian Australasian Line's vessel *"Aorangi."* Mungo followed after the war. Elizabeth gave birth to David in Paddington in 1947, Sonia in Hammersmith in1953, Diana in Hammersmith in1955 and Lorraine in Hammersmith in 1956. When considered that 132 Tildesley Road, Putney housed Mungo Ireland's family consisting of seven in 1965, it becomes clear why *"Harry"* the lodger was considered a burden. (Another mouth to feed etc.) Unfortunately, *"Harry"* like his brother Mungo was not a member of the temperance movement at that time either. Henry Johnstone Ireland was born in Dundee in 1928. He was married in Bedfordshire in 1949. The marriage produced three daughters; one in 1954, one in 1956, (she died two days after her birth) and one in 1958.

Henry Johnstone Ireland with his first wife in 1949. Photograph courtesy of their daughter who doesn't wish to be identified in order to protect her mother's identity.

The marriage soured in 1963 and Henry left home finding himself lodging with Mungo until 1965. After his brother's suicide he moved back to the Midlands and teamed up with Rosa Morris who changed her name to Ireland by deed poll. In 1971 Henry married Rosa in West Bromwich. He died at University Hospital Coventry on 20th June 2008 aged seventy-nine. Rosa had died in1991, while Henry's first wife and two daughters survive him. Mungo and *"Harry"* had seven siblings:

• Mary Ann McLauchlan Ireland, born at 31 Princes Street, Dundee on 20th September 1904 at 8.30pm. She died in childbirth in 1928. (So did the child.)

• Jessie Ireland, a girl born at 48 Crescent Lane, Dundee on 23rd December 1906 at 4.00am.

• David Ireland, born on 29th May 1908.

• John Johnstone Ireland, born at 48 Crescent Lane, Dundee on 18th March 1910. Died 1993.

• James Johnstone Ireland, born at 49 Crescent Lane, Dundee on 16th May 1915. Died 1973.

• Catherine Ireland, born at 61 Crescent Street, Dundee on 18th October 1921 at 1.30pm.

• Isabella Anderson Ireland, born at 61 Crescent Street, Dundee on 18th October 1921 at 3.00pm. (Catherine and Isabella were obviously twins, born one and a half hours apart.)

Mungo's maternal grandparents were Jehoshua Henry Johnstone a ship riveter and Mary Ann Law Johnstone née McLauchlan. Jehoshua was born in February 1861 in the Parish of Minnigaff in west Kirkcudbrightshire and died of cardiac failure in Dundee in1908. Mary his widow who was born at Meal Vennel, Perth in1864 died of aneurism of the aorta in Dundee in1929.

Chapter 9

Another Nudes' Murder Suspect

Over seventy years before the Hammersmith nudes' murders, an unknown serial killer nicknamed *"Jack the Ripper"* had terrorized the East End of London. During a killing spree between August and November 1888, a total of five prostitutes were murdered in the Whitechapel area. All five victims, Mary Ann Nichols aged forty-three, Annie Chapman aged forty-seven, Elizabeth Stride aged forty-five, Catherine Eddowes aged forty-six and Mary Jane Kelly aged twenty-five were believed to be the victims of just one man; *"Jack the Ripper."* It was later believed by the police that the killer of the five Whitechapel victims may also have been responsible for the murders of another six women between 1888 and 1891. Over the years over two hundred works of non-fiction have been published, *"identifying"* the culprit.

Freddie Mills looks on as his wife Chrissie secures a glove on a sparring partner. Photograph courtesy of Southwark Local Studies Library and with the kind help of Freddie's daughter, Susan Mills.

After the killings in the West End area of London stopped in 1965, a number of authors propounded theories as to who *"Jack the Stripper"* was. One of the most prominent candidates put forward was the Bournemouth born boxer Frederick Percival Mills, better known as *"Fearless Freddie."*

On Sunday 4th November 2001 Tony Thompson a crime correspondent with *'The Observer'* newspaper wrote an article highlighting a book that was to be published the following year accusing boxing hero Freddie Mills of *'murdering eight women.'* It is believed that the statement made in John du Rose's 1971 book, *"Murder Was My Business"* about the *"Stripper"* committing suicide which had led to confusion and Mills having the finger pointed at him. He had committed suicide in July 1965. It is difficult to see how the confusion arose because John du Rose specifically stated that his suspect had committed suicide *'within a month of the murder of Bridget O'Hara'*, a murder which took place sometime between January and February 1965. Mills' death occurred five to six months later.

Mills was born on 26th June 1919 at 7 Terrace Road, Bournemouth, one of the most deprived areas of the town at that time. He was the youngest of four children born to Thomas Mills and his wife Lottie Hilda Mills, née Gray, who had married in Christchurch Hampshire in 1907. Freddie attended St Michael's School, Bournemouth until the age of fourteen and then worked as an apprentice milkman. He started his boxing career at the age of ten when his mother bought him his first pair of gloves.

He learned the rudiments of the game sparring with his elder brother Charlie who was himself a boxing professional. Freddie entered a novices' competition at the age of fifteen and won. His first professional fight at the age of sixteen was in 1936 and over the next three years he had many hundreds of small bouts touring with Sam McKeowen's boxing booths.

One of Sam McKeowen's boxing booths. The boxer on the left is Jack "Slugger" Wilkes, an uncle of the author. Photograph courtesy of Len Wilkes, nephew of Jack and a cousin of the author.

Here he honed his skills, seeing off the majority of those that were brave – or foolish enough to take him on. Throughout the next nine years Mills fought his way to the top. On 26th July 1948 he won the title of Light-Heavyweight Champion of the World after defeating American Gus Lesnevich at the White City Stadium, London. He held the title until 24th January 1950, the day that Joey Maxim knocked him out in the tenth round at Earls Court, London.

On 30th September 1948, twenty-nine-year-old Mills married thirty-five-year-old Chrissie Marie McCorkindale at the Methodist Church, Half Moon Lane, Camberwell.

Chrissie was the ex-wife of boxer Donald McCorkindale whom she had married in 1934. She was the daughter of Ted Broadrib (who changed his surname to Broadribb) Mills' boxing manager. Mills inherited a stepson, nine-year-old Donald Edward Hugh McCorkindale from his wife's first marriage.

Donald has now been a well-known actor for over fifty-five years. He was born on 27th January 1939. Freddie and Chrissie went on to have two children of their own, Susan who was born in 1952 and Amanda in 1958. Mills retired from boxing in 1950 but kept himself in the limelight by making walk-on appearances in various films and becoming a presenter on the BBC pop music programme *"Six-Five Special."* In 1947 he became co-owner of Freddie Mills Chinese Restaurant at 143 Charing Cross Road, London, WC2, which in May 1963 was developed into a nightclub, the Freddie Mills Nite Spot.

Freddie Mills Nite Spot is now a William Hill betting office.

He became friends with the now notorious Kray twins who regularly frequented the club. The business was a success at first, but owing in part to undercover operations by a Fleet Street newspaper, Mills' empire was about to crash.

On 5th July 1964 the *'People'* newspaper accused Freddie Mills of using the club as a front for providing sexual services and the headline screamed: *'It's time you cleaned up your club, Mr Mills.'* The stress brought upon Mills by the bad publicity and by the numerous police raids on his premises took its toll. Added to this he suffered from insomnia and bouts of headaches, no doubt brought on by years of taking blows to the head in the boxing ring. Mills had also been stressed over ill feelings towards him by tenants he had evicted from a property he owned at Stanstead Road, Forest Hill. He had evicted four families in order to sell it to raise desperately needed capital.

The day before his death, Mills and his business partner at the Nite Spot, Andrew Chin Guan Ho of Hertsbourne End, Bushey Heath, Hertfordshire had appeared before Marlborough Street Magistrates' Court in connection with an earlier police raid on the club. They had both been fined £50 with 18 guineas costs. Mills and Ho had been charged with supplying liquor to persons not taking a proper meal and allowing the premises, to which the public had access, to be used for gaming on a fruit machine. Mills had told the court that sandwiches were always available for his customers but he hadn't realised that these did not constitute a proper meal. Regarding the fruit machine he said: *'They are supposed to make a fortune, but believe me they don't. I never tried to hide the machine. In fact, when the premises were broken into I told the press that the only property missing was the sixpences from the fruit machine.'* After going home and telling his wife about the fine he was almost in tears when he complained: *'Whatever I try to do I cannot win.'* Chrissie had told him not to worry, as things would get better. But things weren't going to get better. In fact, things were going to get worse. Much worse!

At 4.00pm on the afternoon of Saturday 24th July 1965, Mills, who was recovering from a bout of pneumonia had gone to bed to rest. At 7.30pm he went downstairs for a meal and then complaining of a headache went back to bed. Unable to sleep he got up again to have a coffee and enjoyed dancing *'The Twist'* in the kitchen with seven-year-old Amanda. About 9.30pm he went back upstairs to change into his suit and tie and told Chrissie that he was going to the Nite Spot. He left home at Joggi Villa, 186 Denmark Hill, Camberwell, in his Citroen car, registration number 610 DLR. He drove into Goslett Yard at the rear of his club and parked up.

Freddie Mills' former home at Camberwell.

Mills parked his car in front of the shutter door on the right. The entrance to the rear of his club was through an alley on the left, which is now blocked by a steel gate.

Mills had been expected to host a cabaret at the club, which normally started at around midnight. He told an employee, Robert Anthony Deacon, who had seen him in Goslett Yard, that he had had a drink and he was going to sleep it off in the car. Around 1.00am on Sunday 25th July, Henry John Grant, the head waiter at the Nite Spot found Mills slumped in the rear seat of his car and thinking Mills had been taken ill reported the matter to the club co-owner Mr Ho.

Shortly afterwards, Mills' wife and stepson Donald and his wife turned up at the club and were told by Ho: '*Something is wrong with Freddie.*' Chrissie ordered Ho to phone for an ambulance which he did and when he returned to the car, she said: '*Oh, Andy, Freddie has shot himself,*' and pointed to a gun in the vehicle. While the ambulance was on its way Mark Chelliah, a barman at the Nite Spot arrived on the scene. Mark and Donald later both made police statements that when they looked into the Citroen they saw a .22 fairground rifle propped against Mills' right leg with the muzzle pointing upwards. Shortly afterwards the ambulance arrived and removed Mills to the Middlesex Hospital where he was seen by Dr Jowett and was declared '*dead on arrival.*' Her doctor heavily sedated Chrissie who went into shock after the incident. Owing to the nature of Mills' death and more probably because of who Mills was, the area around Goslett Yard soon swarmed with high-ranking police officers who carried out a thorough investigation into the death. The officers included Detective Chief Inspector Wallace Virgo, Detective Inspector Harold Walton, Detective Inspector Draper, Detective Inspector Robertson, Detective Sergeant Dennis, and Detective Sergeant Adams of C3 Branch. Also on hand was Detective Sergeant Lawrence, Laboratory Liaison Officer.

Recovered from Mills' car were two empty .22 shell cases. It seemed apparent that Mills had tested what damage would be done with the gun by firing one shot into the nearside front door of his car. The shot went through the interior skin of the door but failed to come out of the outer skin although a clear dent was made. Mills was now sure that a second bullet he had reserved for himself would do the job he intended, to take his own life. Although it has to be acknowledged that shooting oneself above the eyelid is a very unusual act it has also to be recognised that owing to the nature of the type of shot in fairground rifles, Freddie Mills would have been concerned that by shooting himself in any other part of the hard boned head, he may have only caused serious injury and not gained the desired results.

At Westminster Mortuary, Horseferry Road, SW1, Professor Cedric Keith Simpson carried out a one hour and twenty minute post-mortem on Mills' body, beginning at 6.00am on Sunday 25th July. He noted: '*Contact wound by direct contact of the rifle muzzle in the corner of the right eye, so preventing burning – the muzzle going right into the eye. Slug calibre not powerful enough to create an exit wound. Reach of 34ins., - 23ins. being sufficient to fire the gun…. Passage of bullet: Direction – just below horizontal and slightly inwards. Shattering into minute fragments. Because of the thick bone the shot had to penetrate at the base of the skull.*' Professor Simpson concluded: '*There is nothing from the medical examination of this wound or of the body generally to give cause for suspicion of foul play. In the site of election and the direction of discharge the wound shows nothing out of keeping with deliberate self-infliction.*'

Detective Sergeant Gordon Harris of the Flying Squad had ascertained that the gun found in Mills' car had belonged to the owner of a rifle range at Battersea funfair, Mrs May Gladys Ronaldson of 316 Queenstown Road, Wandsworth. She told DS Harris that she had known Mills for over thirty years and had looked upon him as one of the family. She said Mills had visited her on Tuesday 20th July 1965 to borrow a fairground rifle as he had been asked to dress as a cowboy to appear at a fête in Esher, Surrey. He returned the gun two days later on 22nd July claiming the fête had been cancelled owing to the weather. Mills had called again on Mrs Ronaldson the following day, Friday 23rd July to borrow the gun again saying the fête had been re-scheduled for the next day.

While Mrs Ronaldson made Mills a cup of tea he discreetly pocketed three live rounds of ammunition that had been left on the kitchen mantelpiece. Mrs Ronaldson had not been aware that Freddie had taken them until she had learned of the shooting. As soon as she had realised the ammunition had been taken she contacted the police after which she identified the gun as the one she had loaned Mills. When it was examined at the police laboratory at New Scotland Yard it was certified that the two spent cartridges found in Mills' car and one unspent cartridge found in the breech of the rifle were of the same batch as two other live rounds that Mills had left on Mrs Ronaldson's mantelpiece.

Professor Cedric Keith Simpson CBE, MD, FRCP, FRC-Path, MA, LLD, DMJ. (1907-1985.)
Professor Simpson was the first Professor of Forensic Medicine at the University of London and was one of the foremost forensic pathologists of the twentieth century. He became famous through his involvement in many notorious murder trials, including that of John George Haigh, (the Acid Bath Killer in 1949), Ronald Kray, (who shot and killed George Cornell in the Blind Beggar Public House, Whitechapel, in 1966), and John Reginald Halliday Christie (of 10 Rillington Place who was hanged in 1953. He had murdered at least six people and has since been implicated in the murders of two others). Professor Simpson was also involved with the Bethnal Green Station disaster victims. On 3rd March 1943 the station that was being used as an air raid shelter was the scene of Britain's worst civilian disaster of the Second World War. A woman tripped on the staircase of the station, which created a domino effect with 300 people falling and being crushed. 173 men, women and children lost their lives. Photograph courtesy of Dr Neville Davis MBE, Hon Secretary of the Medico-Legal Society.

Chrissie Mills told the police that her husband had never mentioned anything to her about a fête or a charity performance at Esher. She said that in the past he had dressed as a cowboy for a charity performance with Billy Smart's Circus, but he had certainly not gone to Esher on the Saturday that he had died. She said her son Donald had taken her husband aside shortly before his death to get him to say what was on his mind following a three-month bout of depression. Mills had confided in Donald that things were getting on top of him, especially the fact that the Nite Spot, which was now his only source of income, was in dire trouble.

Donald McCorkindale of 20 Rutland Court, Denmark Hill, London, told the police that he had last seen his stepfather alive at 2.30pm on Saturday 24th July 1965 at his mother's address. He said Freddie *"was in a mood,"* which was not unusual. He said that around 11.15pm he and his wife (Kathleen, whom he had married a few months previously) were enjoying drinks at the Opera Tavern opposite Drury Lane Theatre with fellow actor Nicholas Henson. (Some of Henson's most notable television roles include *'Fawlty Towers,' 'A Touch of Frost,' 'Eastenders'* and *'The Bill.'*) McCorkindale, his wife and Henson then went to the dressing room of actor Paul Daneman at the Drury Lane Theatre and enjoyed drinks with him. (Daneman's credits include *'Zulu,' 'The Saint,' 'The Professionals'* and *'Rumpole of the Bailey.'*) McCorkindale said that after leaving the theatre at about 11.50pm he went about a few tasks before returning to his mother's home where he stayed until about 12.35am. He, his wife and his mother then went on to the Nite Spot where they learned the dreadful news of Mills' death. He told the police: *'I saw that my stepfather was in the rear offside seat, sitting upright as though he was asleep. My mother went to the car and opened the nearside rear door and got into the car, shook him; put her arms around his neck. She started to cry and I dragged her away.'*

The funeral of Freddie Mills was organised by boxing promoter Jack Solomons. It took place on Friday 30th July 1965 and it was estimated that over 2,000 people turned up at the parish church of St Giles, Camberwell. A huge wreath from Solomons summed it all up. It read: *"Freddie the Greatest, Freddie the Real Champ, Freddie, always the Gentleman."* On the catafalque, which was surrounded with flowers, was a heart of red roses which bore the message, *"Broken."* It was from Freddie's wife Chrissie who was indeed broken. The list of stars from the world of boxing and showbusiness that attended the funeral read like a Who's Who. Bruce Forsyth gave the funeral address and was also one of the pallbearers, as was English Heavyweight boxer Henry Cooper. (Now Sir Henry Cooper OBE, KSG.) Other boxers who attended were: Terry Downes, (World Middleweight Title, 1961), Al Phillips, (European Featherweight Title, 1947), Dick Richardson from Maesglas, Newport, (European Heavyweight Title, March 1960 to June 1962), and Johnny Williams, (Heavyweight British and Empire Titles, 1952).

In giving the funeral address, Bruce Forsyth said: *'My task is easy because I am talking about Freddie. He was a great sportsman, a great showbusiness personality. But what was he like underneath? I know you are asking that…. All I can say is, if you ask anyone who knew him they would say, "A great guy" or "A nice fellow." To be loved in two very tough professions as boxing and showbusiness is a very, very rare thing. Part of the reason he was loved was because he loved kids. He did a lot of things for kids anywhere. He did not do it for publicity. He just loved them.'*

After a brief prayer the funeral cortège slowly wound its way towards Camberwell New Cemetery for Freddie's burial.

The inquest into Mills' death was held without a jury at Westminster Coroner's Court on August 2nd 1965, just five weeks after his demise. Pathologist, Professor Cedric Keith Simpson said that he was of the opinion that Mills had fired a single bullet from a fairground rifle into his right eye, which led to the shot spinning around in his skull causing irreparable damage inside the head. A steady stream of witnesses gave their version of events surrounding the discovery of Mills' body. The coroner Dr Gavin Thurston concluded the inquest with the words: *'I have no doubt that it was a deliberate action. Mills died from a firearm wound to the head. This was self-inflicted, so he killed himself.'* Dr Thurston recorded a verdict of suicide. It had been assumed that Mills who had led the high life could not cope with the thought of being reduced to poverty which appeared was coming his way after the perceived crash of his business.

The funeral of Freddie Mills. Circled, left, Bruce Forsyth and right Henry Cooper. The cost of reproducing this Getty Image photograph sponsored by Chat magazine.

Many unfounded rumours have circulated about Freddie Mills since his death; one being that he killed himself following depression brought about by the death of his friend, singer Michael Holliday. Holliday had released a number of songs including two number one hit singles, *'The Story of My Life'* in 1958 and *'Starry Eyed'* in 1959. He had reputedly suffered from stage fright, which led to a mental breakdown and his eventual suicide in October 1963. Some have claimed that Mills and Holliday were homosexuals.

More sinister claims have been circulated that Mills was disposed of by the Kray twins or by a Chinese triad gang intent on muscling in on the Nite Spot. (It seems odd that anyone would want to take over a dying business!) More than one person has claimed that Mills committed suicide because he knew he was on the verge of being arrested for the Hammersmith nudes' murders.

Following growing rumours that Mills had been murdered by the Kray twins, the Criminal Investigation Department at New Scotland Yard made further investigations into his death. It had been rumoured that the Krays had killed Mills because he refused to pay them protection money. Mr Andrew Chin Guan Ho who had been Mills' business partner since 1947, told the police that there was no substance whatsoever in the claims that he or Mills had been pressured by the Krays or any other person to pay protection money. He was adamant that in his opinion Mills had killed himself because he was depressed over his financial situation and that their business was failing.

Entering the grounds of the Coroner's Court is, left Freddie Mills' business partner Andy Ho and right the head waiter at Freddie Mills Nite Spot, Henry John Grant. © Mirrorpix.

Andy Ho was himself an actor. He was born Ho Chin Guan in Singapore in 1913. From the 1950s to the 1980s he had appeared in more than fifty films and television programmes including *'You Only Live Twice'*, *'It Ain't Half Hot Mum'* and *'Z Cars.'* He died in Surrey in 1992.

Freddie Mills sparring with his mate, Norman Wisdom, later Sir Norman Joseph Wisdom (4th February 1915 – 4th October 2010). Norman had been unable to attend Freddie's funeral. Photograph courtesy of Len Wilkes, Greenford, London.

Mrs May Gladys Ronaldson the owner of the suicide weapon, was also adamant that Mills had not been the victim of extortionists. She said she had been very close to him and if he had been at all threatened he would have confided in her. Like Mills' business partner she also said that Mills had been depressed and that part of the problem was he thought that he was being forgotten by the public, having once been a worldwide celebrity. (Mrs Ronaldson who was born in 1900 died in 1990.)

In 1961 Mills had told a reporter from the South London Observer: *'What have I got out of my life? A wife and family, an actor stepson, [Don McCorkindale] and a cauliflower ear. I have enjoyed every minute of it. I am a lucky guy.'* "Lucky Guy" Freddie had been the hero of Camberwell. He loved being waylaid into giving his autograph and was always ready to lend a hand in opening fêtes. Ironically he had been actively involved in the St Giles Centre Camberwell, an organization that sought to help *"potential suicides and others in distress."*

On 9th October 1968, over three years after Mills' death, Detective Sergeant R Deacon concluded in his re-investigation report: *'From enquiries made there is no evidence to suggest that Freddie Mills was murdered and the circumstances of his death as set out on correspondence No. 201/65/112, are without doubt an accurate account of the incident. I have discussed the matter with Detective Superintendent Virgo, the officer who dealt with the matter and during the course of his investigations he could find no evidence that the Krays or any other person was demanding protection money from Mills, respecting his club known as Freddie Mills Nite Spot, 143 Charing Cross Road, WC2. The Kray twins and some of their hangers-on had visited the club and had in fact been photographed with Mills, but it is a well known fact that the Krays delighted in having their photographs taken with well known personalities and particularly with persons connected with boxing.'*

The rumours still abound. The above mentioned Detective Superintendent Harold Virgo, formerly Detective Chief Inspector, who had concluded his original investigation into the death of Freddie Mills with a written report dated 20th August 1965 said: *'No evidence was found to suggest foul play…. The origin of the .22 rifle used was traced as a result of information received from Detective Sergeant Harris…. He told me Mills had obtained the rifle from Mrs May Gladys Ronaldson…. I made arrangements to see her on 26th July 1965, in company with Detective Sergeant Harris.'*

A copy of Virgo's signature at the end of his written report.

Detective Superintendent Virgo! Detective Sergeant Harris! Surely not Detective Chief Superintendent Wallace Harold Virgo, later Commander at Scotland Yard and Detective Sergeant Gordon Harris of the Flying Squad? Surely they are! What credence can now be given to their evidence, with the knowledge that allegations against these two men later almost brought Scotland Yard to its knees with revelations of corruption at the highest level? On Saturday 29th March 1969 Harris aged thirty-nine hit the front page of *'The Times'* when it was revealed that he had planted a stick of Gelignite on petty criminal Michael Roy Perry. He then accused Perry of unlawfully possessing the Gelignite, offering to drop the matter if Perry paid a back-hander. Harris was also accused of accepting a £25 bribe from Perry for showing favour to him in connection with a prosecution for dishonestly handling twelve bottles of stolen whisky.

Two reporters from *'The Times'* newspaper had secretly taped various meetings held between Harris and Perry discussing bribes. After handing their evidence to Scotland Yard, a three year police inquiry led to Harris appearing at the Old Bailey charged with conspiracy, corruptly accepting money and demanding money with menaces. After a seven-week trial at which he had pleaded not guilty to various charges he was found guilty. Mr Justice Shaw commended Detective Chief Superintendent Alfred Moody for his efficiency in investigating the case and securing a prosecution. On Friday 3rd March 1972 Harris was jailed for six years.

It gets worse! Five years later, in March 1977, fifty-nine-year-old Virgo, Harris' former boss, also hit the national newspaper headlines. He stood trial at the Old Bailey charged with conspiring with others to extort money from persons who were involved in the vice trade in the West End of London during the period 1964-1972. The vice trade! Didn't the *'People'* newspaper of 5th July 1964 accuse Freddie Mills of being involved in the vice trade? It now seems ironic that extortionist Virgo had been put in charge of an investigation probing whether or not Mills had been the victim of extortionists. If Virgo had been on the Krays' payroll and if the Krays were behind Mills' death because he refused to pay protection money, what a cover having Virgo in charge of the inquiry.

Wallace Harold Virgo of Horse Lane Orchard, Ledbury, Hereford, who was born on 11th September 1917, was jailed in May 1977 for twelve years for receiving bribes which totalled £60,000. (Worth approx. £334,000 in 2011.)

A fact that would have made the Queen's hair curl was the revelation that Her Majesty, had in 1971 awarded Commander Virgo of the London Metropolitan Police, the QPM (Queen's Police Medal) for distinguished service in the police force. In his thirty-six year police career he had received twenty-five commendations. He had been a former head of Scotland Yard's Murder Squad and had been heavily involved with Scotland Yard's Obscene Publications Squad. Later, after service in other parts of the force he returned to Scotland Yard with the rank of Commander with the Obscene Publications Squad. He had at one time been in charge of the 3,500 detectives in the London Metropolitan Police. With his position he could have stamped out the corruption that he knew was taking place within the Obscene Publications Squad. Instead he wholeheartedly and greedily joined in. Virgo had provided protection to those involved in the pornography trade – at a cost. If they paid, the police wouldn't raid them. Virgo also sold obscene publications to dealers for half the normal price, if they *"played the game."* These were publications confiscated from pornography dealers who refused to pay protection money.

And there's more! Another officer who had attended Goslett Yard after Mills' death was also involved in the 1977 corruption trial. According to pornography dealer Ronald Mason, in 1969 Inspector Robertson of the Obscene Publications Squad, had raided his shop in Dean Street, Soho and found pornographic material. Another corrupt officer had told Mason that Robertson would *"play"* in return for a £14,000 cash bribe. The corrupt officer? Detective Chief Inspector Alfred Moody, the earlier mentioned receiver of commendation. Five years after the commendation Moody was now in the dock with Virgo and four other crooked cops. Like Virgo, fifty-one-year-old Moody also received a twelve-year prison sentence. Virgo and Moody were told by Mr Justice Mars-Jones: *'This is a case in which thousands and thousands of pounds have been involved, and I am going to make sure that if any of that money is still around it will be put towards the cost of the defence.'* He ordered that Moody pay £10,000 costs and Virgo £15,000. A fact that would have stuck in the gut of many was that Virgo was sent to Leyhill open prison in

Gloucestershire. It appeared to some that he was still pulling the strings. If that wasn't enough, he appealed against his conviction on a technicality. On 15th March 1978 his appeal was heard by Lord Justice Geoffrey Lane who handed down the puzzling and highly controversial decision that Virgo be set free. Virgo then had the audacity to ask if he could be given back the £15,000 he had been ordered to pay towards his defence costs by Mr Justice Mars-Jones ten months earlier. His request was denied.

Wallace Harold Virgo QPM, with his wife Winifred and thirty-seven-year-old daughter Margaret after his release from prison. Virgo died in Bristol in November 1990 aged seventy-three. He had married Winifred Palmer Gilbert in Hereford in 1939. She died in Bristol in 1993 aged seventy-four. The cost of reproducing this Mirrorpix photograph sponsored by Stan Challenger, Step By Step Carpets, Brynmawr.

Reginald Kray had been sentenced to life imprisonment on 5th March 1969 for his part in the murder of Jack *"The Hat"* McVitie. He was informed by Mr Justice Melford Stevenson that he would serve a minimum of thirty years; at that time the longest prison sentence ever passed at the Old Bailey for murder. Thirty-one years later in August 2000 he was released from prison on compassionate grounds suffering from terminal cancer. Shortly after his release he was interviewed for a BBC1 documentary. He was asked if there were any killings that he had been involved in for which he hadn't been charged. *'One'* he replied. The documentary was entitled: *"Reggie Kray: The Final Word"* and Kray certainly had the final word on the subject. He refused to enlarge on who the *'One'* was. David Seabrook in his book *"Jack of Jumps"* ponders: *'Why didn't he enlarge? Why keep quiet? Image? If the victim was Freddie Mills, if the fans learned that Ron and Reg murdered sporting heroes as well as criminal lowlifes – well, it would tarnish the image. And image was everything….'* Kray died shortly after the interview (on 1st October 2000) and took his secret to the grave.

Author David Seabrook a strapping, healthy, forty-eight-year-old was found dead in bed at his flat in Canterbury after a break-in by Kent police officers in January 2009. Seabrook had caused a huge amount of anguish to relatives of the Hammersmith nudes' victims with the uncaring way he had written about the victims in his book *"Jack of Jumps."* He also embarrassed Scotland Yard, tarring them all with the same brush as Harold Virgo and his cronies. Already, conspiracy theories abound regarding Seabrook's sudden death. He would have loved it.

Freddie Mills had the dubious honour of having two burials. After his first burial, members of the public and many of his fans for months afterwards looked upon his grave as a shrine. Some took flowers away as trophies. Some took flasks and sandwiches to have a picnic at his graveside.

The *'People'* newspaper took up the disgusting acts that were committed by so-called friends and fans of Freddie. It quoted Reverend Stewart Carne-Ross as saying: *'It is appalling what has been happening. Parents bring their children here for a day out. They come here to have picnics and poke morbidly round the grave.'* Eleven months after Mills' original burial his remains were exhumed and buried in a different part of the cemetery. This was done in response to the British Board of Boxing Control's objection to the disgraceful way that many persons had behaved at the cemetery.

Freddie's grave at Camberwell New Cemetery.

Chrissie Mills lived to the ripe old age of eighty. She died on 4th November 1994 in Lewisham, five miles away from the home that she had shared with Freddie for seventeen years. Her cremated remains were buried with Freddie at Camberwell.

She was originally named Chrissy (because of being born on Christmas day?) on 25th December 1913 by Edward Alfred (Ted) and Maria Broadrib née Dobbs, who had married in 1909. Chrissie's parents also had three other daughters; Lily in 1911, Margaret in 1912 and Grace in 1916.

Chrissie, who had originally believed that her husband had committed suicide, later made her feelings clear that she was convinced that he had been murdered. Freddie Mills, who had a genuine love for children and cared about the disadvantaged, founded the Freddie Mills Boxing Club at Grosvenor Terrace, Camberwell, about 1962. Since 1992 John and Lesley Scanlon and Bob and Linda Cheeseman have run it as volunteers.

They care for the welfare of many of the disadvantaged and handicapped in the area and raise funds for trips and parties for them. Susan Mills, who was thirteen when her father died, today runs a dancing class for the elderly at the Freddie Mills Boxing Club. Amanda Mills who was seven in 1965 lives in Ireland. Donald McCorkindale is still active in the acting profession.

Some of the present day members of the Freddie Mills Boxing Club proudly wearing their Freddie Mills tee shirts. Pictured rear row left to right are: Tony Johnson – Tony Collins – Leslie Burnham – Jimmy Clark – Jason Alder. Front row left to right are: Dean Proud – Richard Issey – Matthew Issey – Terry Agnew (club helper) Photograph taken June 2009, kindly provided by Pat Davies.

Chapter 10

Grasping at Straws

Another suspect (whose name is withheld) put forward as possibly being *"Jack the Stripper"* was a former officer with the London Metropolitan Police.

In February 1972 journalist Owen Summers wrote a series of articles for the *'Sun'* newspaper dealing with theories that had previously been bandied around regarding the alleged culprit. Summers decried John du Rose's claim in 1971 that the former night security patrolman (Mungo Ireland), who had committed suicide in 1965, was the killer. Like Seabrook, Summers claimed that this suspect had been working in Scotland when at least one of the nudes' murders took place.

Summers also claimed that he had recently conferred with a number of senior police officers who had worked on the nudes' murders and the consensus of opinion was that du Rose had been barking up the wrong tree when he had made his claims about the suicide suspect. Summers then makes assumptions that the *"Stripper"* could *possibly* have been the earlier mentioned former police officer who would have had intimate knowledge of how the police operation to find the killer worked, thereby keeping one step ahead of his colleagues.

The officer he alluded to had joined the London Metropolitan Police in 1956 but in September 1962 he was suspended from duties and charged with a series of breaking and entering incidents at a number of business premises. At his trial he had pleaded guilty to numerous offences and told the court that the reason why he had committed the crimes was because he had been dissatisfied with the way he had been treated by his former colleagues at Kensington and Hammersmith police stations. He said his intention was not to steal for material gain but to frustrate his fellow officers by keeping one step ahead of them and running circles around them. He felt that by committing crimes that his colleagues couldn't solve, it would make them seem as incompetent as they had made him feel. He was jailed for a year and dismissed from the Met.

After finishing his sentence in 1963, did the disgruntled gamekeeper turned poacher become even further dissatisfied with his lot in life? To some it appeared that way. The facts are that shortly after his release from prison the first of the so-called *"Jack the Stripper"* killings began. By playing around with figures and adding two and two together, senior police officers deduced that the six definite nudes' murders victims, (Tailford to O'Hara) were dumped at four separate police sub-divisions where their disgruntled ex-fellow officer had worked. He was pursued relentlessly, such was the desperation shown by the police to catch their man. After repeated questioning of the suspect, Detective

Superintendent William Baldock, the senior officer in charge, concluded that his theory may after all have been just a theory.

But the plot thickens! David Seabrook in his book *"Jack of Jumps"* (published by Granta in 2006) says on page 363: '*Well, bad things, like good things, must come to an end. That's life I suppose, and it doesn't mean you have to kill yourself. So let's just say: The suspect did not kill himself. He is not dead.*' The suspect here mentioned is the policeman cum burglar who apparently was still alive in 2008 aged seventy-two.

In a review of *"Jack of Jumps"* writer Stewart Home praises Seabrook's impressive research and layout of his book but criticized him for failing to finger the killer. In the review entitled; *"Put Up or Shut Up: David Seabrook at the Last Chance Saloon,"* Home identified and named the still alive ex-cop but added: '*I must stress here that there is no smoking gun. Detective Superintendent William Baldock who investigated AJ *******... in the end failed to build a case against the suspect.*' Home claimed that Seabrook had confided in him at the launch party for Tom McCarthy's book *"Remainder"* that the *"Stripper"* was still alive and was named in *"Jack of Jumps."* (The suspect wasn't named but was alluded to. It was Home, who through his own research found out the suspect's identity and named him in *his* review.)

The plot thickens further. Another former Metropolitan Police Officer is now added to the list of suspects. Home continues: '*The police files on "Jack the Stripper" remain closed to the public, and yet Seabrook was granted access to them; which naturally raises the question as to why he was allowed to review this material. Among other things, it seems likely that the "old bill" did not like the ongoing speculation about the identity of "Jack the Stripper" which for the past thirty-five years has tended to implicate serving or retired Met officers. Indeed a more recent theory to do the rounds was one to be found in Jimmy Evans' and Martin Short's book "The Survivor" (Mainstream, Edinburgh 2001), which named deceased top cop Detective Chief Superintendent Tommy Butler as the nude murderer....That said, I would assume members of the Metropolitan Police Force would much prefer having a low-ranking officer, who was dismissed from the service in 1962, identified as the killer, to a top cop like Butler; which might explain why Seabrook was granted access to the closed police files.*'

In his acknowledgements in *"Jack of Jumps"* Seabrook wrote: '*I have benefited enormously from the kindness of the Metropolitan Police, who granted me access to all the available files relating to the nudes' murders.... These files are closed to public inspection; David Capus of Metropolitan Police Records Management informs me that they will remain closed for '100 years from the date of the last active minute.' I would like to thank David Capus and his colleagues Andrew Brown and Alan Oakley for their assistance in making the files available to me, and for the patience and courtesy with which they dealt with my many queries.*'

Mystery piles upon mystery! In an email sent to the author of *"Who was Jack the Stripper?"* on 9th September 2008, David Capus writes: '*Concerning the book "Jack of Jumps" by Mr David Seabrook. In the introduction he gives the impression to the reader that I permitted him access to the Metropolitan Police case files; this is not true. The fact is that during the course of my correspondence with Mr Seabrook I consistently refused him access to the files. Subsequently I understand that he approached another unit within this service and was granted access to the files by them. I am not able to say why or under what terms he was granted this access, but it was done without the consent of either myself or any of my colleagues within the Metropolitan Police Records Branch, where responsibility for authorising the release of the information from records in the custody of the National Archives ultimately rests. Why Mr Seabrook should attribute this disclosure to me I can only speculate.'* The email was received four months *before* Seabrook's sudden death, so it was not a case of David Capus trying to cover himself after Seabrook died and couldn't answer for himself.

According to Frank Quinn who was born in May 1964 to murder victim number seven, Frances Brown, he and David Seabrook had many telephone conversations while Seabrook was researching for his book. He told Frank that his original research had been into the death of boxer Freddie Mills. Frank said that Seabrook had told him that he had viewed all the original information relating to Mills' death, which was stored at Hendon Police College at Aerodrome Road, Colindale, London. While at Hendon, Seabrook became aware that all the original files relating to the Hammersmith nudes' murders were also stored there. Apparently he spent four months at Hendon studying them, which resulted in him publishing his controversial book, *"Jack of Jumps."*

29 Hestercombe Avenue, Fulham. (arrowed) Photograph early 1970s courtesy of Hammersmith and Fulham Archives and Local History Centre.

Aldensley Road Hammersmith. Harold Jones lived in the last house on the right from 1966-1971. Photograph early 1970s courtesy of Hammersmith and Fulham Archives and Local History Centre.

Chapter 11

"Jack the Stripper" Unmasked

Would the real *"Jack the Stripper"* please step forward!

In May 2008, the author of this book published a true crime story entitled: *"Every Mother's Nightmare - Abertillery in Mourning."* For the benefit of those who have not read that publication, a part of this chapter, most of chapter twelve and parts of chapter thirteen are a condensed version of the seventeen chapters of that book. It dealt in depth with the murders in Abertillery, south Wales, of two schoolchildren, Freda Burnell aged eight and Florence Irene Little aged eleven. These ghastly murders were committed in 1921 and the perpetrator, fifteen-year-old Harold Jones was released from prison in 1941 after having served twenty years for his crimes. Included in the book were Jones' movements up until his death in 1971. On page 107 of the book it states: In 1947 Harold Jones using his birth name was registered as living at 29 Hestercombe Avenue, Fulham, London.

Also living at that address were George and Eileen Crowe and John Widdows and his daughter Muriel. In 1948 Jones married Kensington born Muriel and he was then registered on the electoral roll as *'Harry Stevens.'* He falsely claimed, on his marriage certificate, that Stevens was his father's surname, when in fact it was his mother's maiden name. Jones' wife gave birth to a child at Fulham Borough Maternity Home in 1950 and the family continued to live in Hestercombe Avenue until 1962.

There is no record in the Hammersmith and Fulham electoral roll of Jones living in that borough between 1963 and 1965. 29 Hestercombe Avenue, between these dates, is recorded as being unoccupied. Presumably Jones still owned that property but was living in an unknown location.

Then from 1966 until his death on 2nd January 1971 he and his family lived at 51 Aldensley Road, Hammersmith. Jones aged sixty-five had died from Carsinomatosis.

At the time of his death he was registered on the electoral roll as *'Harry Jones.'* His death certificate named him as *'Harold Jones, otherwise Harry Stevens.'* According to Anne Wheeldon, the Archivist at the Hammersmith and Fulham Archives and Local History Centre, the rates book lists the occupier of 29 Hestercombe Avenue, Fulham, from 1st April 1962 to 4th June 1962 as John Widdows, the father-in-law of Harold Jones.

Widdows certainly could not have been the occupier as he had died in the first quarter of 1961. So someone was paying the rates in his name for between fifteen and eighteen months after he had died – someone named Harry Stevens! From 4th June 1962 to 31st March 1964 the rates book records the property as empty, no rates being paid. The name Rayners Estate Office is entered in the column describing the property as *"House."*

Jones is buried at Hammersmith (New) Cemetery in the unmarked plot between the two graves forefront. His grave is just a short distance away from where the 8th nudes' victim Bridget O'Hara is buried. Also just a short distance away, is where the 2nd nudes' victim Gwynneth Rees was found buried at the rubbish dump.

In September 2007 following the author supplying information to the Hammersmith police, the London Metropolitan Police Homicide and Serious Crime Command Review Team started investigating the possibility that Harold Jones may have been involved in serious criminal activities in the London area and in Wales on account of the fact that he had been using a variety of aliases after his release from prison in 1941.

After ascertaining that Harold Jones the murderer and Harold Jones/Harry Stevens/ Harry Jones was one and the same person an intense three month investigation was carried out. A letter received by the author from a member of the Review Team on 6th December 2007 read:

Dear Neil
Re: Harold Jones

'Thank you for all your assistance in this matter, the information you have provided has proved to be very helpful. My enquiries are now complete and have led me to conclude that Harold Jones would have presented a danger to young girls throughout his life…. All relevant information has now been presented to South Wales Police, Major Crime Review Unit, who are currently in the process of making further inquiries into the murder of Muriel Drinkwater. Thank you once again and I wish you every success with your forthcoming publication.' Paul.

Muriel Joan Drinkwater, a twelve-year-old schoolgirl had been raped and shot dead in an isolated spot at Penllergaer, near Swansea on 27th June 1946. The killer left his DNA at the scene and Scotland Yard and the family of Jones' second Welsh murder victim,

Florence Irene Little aged eleven, believed that Jones may have been responsible for Muriel's murder. The DNA sample was sent to Forensic Science Services in Chepstow, Gwent, to enhance the profile with a view to identifying Muriel's killer. This was a scientific first as the sample came from the world's oldest crime scene stain. In November 2008 South Wales Police announced that the profiling had been successfully completed and scientists had been able to retrieve a DNA profile from clothing that Muriel had been wearing at the time of her murder in 1946.

Regarding this scientific breakthrough, television, radio and newspapers worldwide covered the story. On Saturday 8th November 2008 a double page feature appeared in the *'Daily Express'* and the *'International Express.'* The article by Adrian Lee included a photograph of Muriel Drinkwater with the caption: *'This girl was the victim of Britain's oldest unsolved murder.'* Next to Muriel was a photograph of Harold Jones with the caption: *'Is modern science about to name this man as her killer?'* Apparently the police have a list of around fifty potential suspects in the Drinkwater case. They refused to confirm whether Harold Jones was one of the suspects and at the time of the publishing of this book no further police announcements have been made regarding the situation.

The *'Times Online'* of 23rd March 2009 claimed that they had learned that the murder review teams from the South Wales and Kent police forces had liaised over the deaths of Muriel Drinkwater and Sheila Martin aged eleven from Fawkham Green, Dartford, who was raped and strangled on 7th July 1946, just ten days after Muriel's murder. The *'Times Online'* claimed that the police had found peculiarities in the sexual assault in the Kent murder, which were also present in the Welsh case.

On 30th March 2010 the *'Times Online'* announced that the police files on the Muriel Drinkwater and Sheila Martin murders which are held at the National Archives at Kew have been declared exempt from disclosure under the Freedom of Information Act. The *'Times Online'* quoted an unnamed police source as saying, (regarding Neil Milkins): *"We have a real problem with amateur sleuths in this area. There are far too many retired people out there who want to write books about unsolved murders, trawling through these records and coming up with half-baked theories. This can cause unnecessary distress to families."*

There we go! Let's all start fretting over whether families of murderers who killed seventy years ago might be upset. Why not change the names of Peter Tobin and Peter Sutcliffe in order to avoid embarrassment whenever their names are mentioned. What about Muriel Drinkwater's family? Claire Philips, Muriel's great-niece told the Western Mail newspaper in November 2008: *"This turned the family upside down and has been talked about through the generations…. This was a terrible, terrible crime that someone has got away with for many decades. We would like to have justice for Muriel at long last."*

Justice on Its Way?

Following the author's appeals through the media and the Internet regarding Jones' whereabouts between 1963 and 1965 an email was received from Mark Buchan Jones of Manchester on 23rd July 2008.

Mark said that his father was named Harold Kenneth Jones after his birth in 1923 but was known as Harold Jones. Owing to the raised eyebrows over the name that was still on the lips of many just a few years after the Abertillery murders, Harold Kenneth Jones was then referred to as Kenneth Jones. Mark said that he had read a story on the

Internet appealing for information about Harold Jones the killer. He suggested: *'Have you considered this case?'* http://en.wikipedia.org/wiki/jackthestripper. After connecting to the above website, the following information was gleaned:

"Jack the Stripper" was the nickname given to an unknown serial killer responsible for what came to be known as the London *"nude murders"* between 1964 and 1965 also known as the *"Hammersmith nudes' murders"* or the *"Hammersmith nudes' case"*…. He murdered six – possibly eight prostitutes whose nude bodies were discovered around London or dumped in the River Thames…'

Harold Kenneth Jones and his son Mark Buchan Jones in August 2009.

Hammersmith murders? Harold Jones! Harry Stevens! Harry Jones! Hammersmith! Following the author's study of the numerous books and articles published dealing with the nudes' murders, certain things written led to a gut feeling that Harold Jones may have been involved in the killings. In Seabrook's book *"Jack of Jumps,"* a clue came from the suicide note that was left to his wife by one of the Hammersmith nudes' murders suspects. That suspect was Mungo Ireland the former night patrolman at the Heron Trading Estate, Acton. He had committed suicide in the lock-up garage at Solna Avenue, West Putney, on the night of 2nd – 3rd March 1965, just two months after the last murder victim Bridget O'Hara vanished. Part of his suicide note read: *'I can't stick it any longer…. It may be my fault but not all of it….'* When Ireland stressed that he couldn't stick it any longer, was he referring to the pressure put upon him by DCI John du Rose's press statements about knowing who the killer was? If he was the killer, who else's fault was it?

After reading DCI John du Rose's 1971 book *"Murder Was My Business,"* it became obvious that he was convinced who the culprit was – (Mungo Ireland). Following the instinct that Jones and Ireland may have been involved in the nudes' murders together, a trip to Battersea Heritage Centre, at Lavender Hill, London, produced a startling revelation. The electoral roll for Putney revealed that Harold Jones, still using the alias Harry Stevens, had been registered as living in the Putney district from some time in

1962 until some time in 1965 (the missing years). He certainly had moved by October 1965. His address in Putney was 20 Colinette Road. (Another startling discovery was that Jones was eligible at that time to serve on an assizes jury.)

20 Colinette Road, Putney.

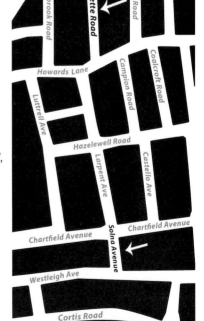

Map showing Colinette Road, Solna Avenue and Tildesley Road, West Putney.

A short walk from Colinette Road and down Larpent Avenue brings you to Mungo Ireland's suicide garage at Solna Avenue. A short walk from there is Ireland's former home at Tildesley Road (see map on previous page). Was this just a coincidence? And is this another one? After Ireland's suicide, Harry Stevens moved and turned up *3.8* miles away at 51 Aldensley Road, Hammersmith. Not only did he change his name to Harry Jones after masquerading for eighteen years as Harry Stevens, but also he was living just two streets away from where the last murder victim, Bridget O'Hara had lived at Agate Road, Hammersmith. He was also two streets away from where the last but one victim Frances Brown had lived at Southerton Road.

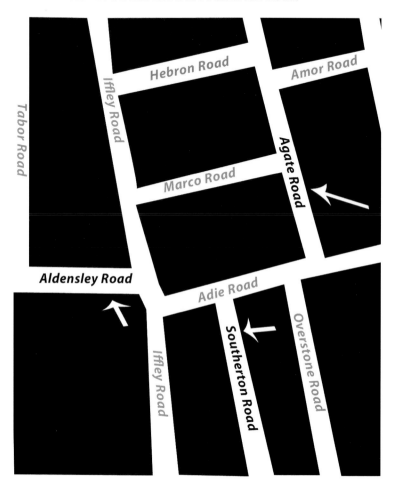

Map showing Aldensley Road, Agate Road, and Southerton Road.

Was this a cynical move? If so, Jones would have delighted in living out his last few years within two streets of his last two victims. Jones had often visited his parents in Abertillery after his release from prison and enjoyed being noticed. He also visited the graves of his two murder victims, Freda Burnell and Florence Little.

No doubt Jones would also have delighted in drinking in the Andover Arms, 57 Aldensley Road, just yards from his home and offering condolences to Michael O'Hara and Paul Quinn. Michael had been the husband of Bridget and Paul had been the partner of Frances Brown.

But why would Jones want to console them for any reason other than wanting to show genuine sympathy? Because the boy psychopath had grown into an adult psychopath!

At 9.30am on Saturday 5th February 1921, Jones attempted to rape and then murdered eight-year-old Freda Burnell in Abertillery. Shortly after darkness fell that afternoon he dumped the body of Freda in a quiet lane just 100 yards from her home. He then callously knocked on her father's door and with pity etched into his face inquired as to whether Freda had been found. Later the same evening he again called at Freda's home and feigned concern for Freda and her family.

In his book *"Jack of Jumps"*, David Seabrook ponders the reason why the nudes' killer stored his victims' bodies in a warehouse, sometimes for weeks, before dumping them at various locations around west London. Harold Jones had done the same with his two murder victims in Abertillery. He had stored eight-year-old Freda Burnell in a warehouse before dumping her body in the lane. Even more disturbing is the fact that he had stored the body of eleven-year-old Florence Little in his own attic after he had killed her until *"the fuss had died down."*

Map showing Hestercombe Avenue and Filmer Road, Fulham.

Was it just a coincidence that the last nudes' murder victim, Bridget O'Hara vanished on 11th January - Jones' birthday - or was she one last birthday present to himself?

Is this another coincidence? On Sunday 19th April 1959, journalist James Cameron of the *'Sunday Pictorial'* interviewed a twenty-five-year-old mother-to-be. The reason for the interview? The woman had placed an advertisement in the window of a south London newsagent's. It read: Young mother-to-be (25) offers unborn baby for sale to good home. Due end of April. Letters only to TF within.

TF appeared to turn out to be a Mrs Theresa Foster of Filmer Road, Fulham. The advert in the shop window had the tongues of the gossipmongers in Fulham wagging furiously. When the story appeared in the *'Sunday Pictorial,'* Theresa Foster's predicament became known nationwide. Those in the streets surrounding Filmer Road would have been drawn to the newspaper article. Those in the next street, Munster Road, would have known and everyone in Hestercombe Avenue, would have known, including the occupant of number 29, Harold Jones aka Harry Stevens (see map on previous page).

But where is there a link between Theresa Foster and Jones? She wasn't one of the eight murdered prostitutes was she? Yes she was! She was victim number three. Woman of many names, Hannah Tailford, murdered five years after the *'Sunday Pictorial'* story.

One year after the *'Sunday Pictorial'* story, the *'Fulham Chronicle'* of 15th April 1960, reported on the jailing of a twenty-six-year-old woman who had stolen a chequebook and driving licence. The woman, from 75 Highbury New Park, Islington, London, had claimed that she had found a paper bag in the gutter at Vanston Place Fulham, which contained the chequebook and licence. Succumbing to temptation she forged a cheque and obtained groceries and cash to the value of £3 from a shop at Dawes Road, Fulham. At West London Magistrates' Court on 9th April 1961 she was sentenced to three months in prison for the theft of the chequebook and licence belonging to Vera Turl. Who was the Islington resident and what had she been doing in Fulham? She never said what she had been doing but she was only a short walk into Harry Stevens' territory in Hestercombe Avenue. The woman's name? Hannah Tailford!

Is the circumstantial evidence presented in this chapter linking Harold Jones to the nudes' murders just a series of coincidences? Sceptics please consider the following:

In 1978 the singing group Boney M had a massive hit with the Brent Dowe and Trevor McNaughton song: *'Rivers of Babylon,'* which remained at number one in the charts for five weeks and charted for a further thirty-five weeks.

The author would contend that the writers didn't pen this song by just plucking words out of the air. They lifted them from a song that was written more than 2,500 years ago! That song by an unknown writer is recorded in the Bible at Psalm 137.

In the King James Version the first 4 verses read:

1 **By the rivers of Babylon, there we sat down, yea we wept, when we remember Zion.**

2 We hanged our harps upon the willows in the midst thereof.

3 **For there they that carried us away captive required of us a song;** and they that wasted us required of us mirth, saying, Sing us one of the songs of Zion.

4 **How shall we sing the Lord's song in a strange land?**

The Boney M version:

1 **By the rivers of Babylon, there we sat down, Yea-eah we wept, when we remember Zion.**

Repeat
2 **When the wicked carried us away in captivity,**
Required from us a song.
How shall we sing the Lord's song in a strange land?
Repeat.

Admittedly not all the verses are identical, but the similarities are remarkable. What do **you** think? (It is not here suggested that Dowe (who died in September 2006) and McNaughton deny basing their song on verses from the Bible.)

Spectacular Events for Jones.

In February 1949, two years after Harold Jones moved to Hestercombe Avenue, a story broke in Fulham that captured the attention of the world's media and Harold Jones. Five hundred yards away from Harold's – at Dawes Road, the police were swarming over a property that featured in the disappearance of two prominent Fulham residents one year earlier.

Dr Archibald Henderson aged fifty-three and his wife Rosalie aged forty-two had apparently vanished without trace on 12th February 1948. The story however started a few years earlier with the disappearance of William Donald McSwan on 9th September 1944. Ten months later William's parents Donald and Amy also vanished. Then on 18th February 1949 a wealthy woman with the remarkably lengthy name of Mrs Henrietta Helen Olivia Robarts Durand-Deacon vanished from the Onslow Court Hotel at South Kensington, where she had been a permanent resident. The police, including Detective Inspector Albert Webb and the then Detective Sergeant John du Rose ('*Four Day Johnny*'), soon suspected another resident who had lived at the hotel for about four years. His name was John George Haigh, and he soon confessed to crimes that shook the world.

John George Haigh, 1909-1949. Haigh had married twenty-one-year-old Beatrice Hamer at Bridlington, Yorkshire on 6th July 1934. The marriage only lasted four months, long enough to produce a daughter Patricia in 1935. This Mirrorpix image sponsored by The Mirrorpix Photo Archives. A history of life in pictures, since 1903. Search more than a century of photos online at www.mirrorpix.com

Haigh told the police that he had lured Mrs Durand-Deacon aged sixty-nine to a warehouse in Leopold Road, Crawley, Sussex where he shot her and dissolved her body in acid. Outside the warehouse, the police took samples from the sludge that Haigh had tipped out of a forty-gallon drum in which he had dissolved his victim. They found remains of a metal handle of a handbag, part of a lipstick container, human gallstones and dentures that had belonged to Mrs Durand-Deacon.

Haigh also told the police that back in 1944 he had invited William Donald McSwan to his then basement at 79 Gloucester Road, hit him on the head and then drained a mug of blood from his neck and drank it. He then put his body in a metal water butt, filled it with acid and dissolved the body. Haigh then told his victim's parents that William had gone away because he had been called up to go into the army against his will. On 2nd July 1945 Haigh then dissolved the bodies of William's parents Donald and Amy after luring them to his basement and killing them. Using forged papers he then sold all of the McSwans property. His total gain was about £4,000. Incredibly, the disappearance of the McSwans was never reported to the police and if Haigh hadn't confessed to the murders, no one would have known what had happened to them to this day. Now back to Dr Henderson and his wife Rosalie.

Doctor Archibald Henderson and his wife Rosalie. © Mirrorpix.

Haigh confessed that he had lured them to the warehouse at Crawley in February 1948, shot them both with Dr Henderson's own gun and dissolved their bodies in acid. He then forged documents and sold their newly acquired property at 16 Dawes Road, Fulham and property elsewhere. Haigh paid more than £7,000 into his bank account in 1948, (worth approx. £170,000 in 2011). Haigh had spent much of his ill earned gains on gambling – and losing. He also told the police that he had murdered a young man by the name of Max, an unnamed woman whom he had met somewhere between Hammersmith Bridge and Hammersmith Broadway and a girl from Eastbourne known only as Mary. Haigh's total score was nine victims if he was to be believed about the last three. He was tried for the murder of Mrs Durand-Deacon on 18th July 1949, entering a plea of insanity. The jury took just fifteen minutes to find him guilty of murder and he was hanged at Wandsworth Prison on 10th August 1949. The goings-on in Fulham in 1949 and Haigh's hanging would surely have thrilled and fascinated Harold Jones.

Here was a true crime story right on his own doorstep. No doubt he would have publicly expressed his revulsion at the killings but in reality he would have loved it.

(In 2000, Glenn Chandler, the creator and writer of the award-winning and highly praised *"Taggart"* series completed writing a two hour drama about John George Haigh, entitled *"A is for Acid."* It was produced by Yorkshire TV, and starred Martin Clunes as Haigh. It was released in 2002.)

The property that the Hendersons bought in July 1947, a toyshop known as The Dolls Hospital. Haigh sold the property to Mr Albert Sydney Somers Clarke in July 1948, five months after murdering the Hendersons. Albert's son-in-law John Smith took over the shop after Albert's death in 1987. The Dolls Hospital eventually closed in 1996 and Mr Smith rented it out until he eventually sold it to Dorothy Blazewicz who owns Dorothy Couture. This modern photograph of 16 Dawes Road is published with the consent of Dorothy Blazewicz.

Somerset Street, Abertillery. Mortimer's Seed Store is the first building on the right.

Chapter 12

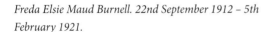

Jones' Antecedents

A t around 9.10am on Saturday 5th February 1921, Harold Jones aged fifteen had served eight-year-old Freda Burnell with a tuppence ha'penny bag of poultry spice at the seed store where he worked for Herbert Henry Mortimer at 90 Somerset Street, Abertillery, Monmouthshire.

Freda Elsie Maud Burnell. 22nd September 1912 – 5th February 1921.

Freda had also asked for a bag of poultry grit in a sealed 10lb bag, but Jones told her that he only had loose grit. Freda said she would return home and ask her father Fred if loose goods would suffice. She failed to return home and Fred searched the area around his residence at 9 Earl Street, Abertillery. Frantically he reported his daughter missing at 1.00pm at the police station just forty yards away from Mortimer's Seed Store. Although Freda had always been an obedient child Fred was hoping that she had just been sidetracked and had perhaps visited a friend. Jones told the police he hadn't noticed whether Freda went left into town or right to Earl Street when she left the shop.

Following an all-night search by thousands of miners and other valley residents, Freda was found the following morning by a workman in a lane at the rear of his home in Duke Street, Abertillery. She had been murdered.

The lane at the rear of Duke Street where Freda's body was found (X marking the spot). Pantypwddyn Road is top right.

On Monday 7th February, two days after the murder, three Scotland Yard detectives arrived in Abertillery to pursue investigations along with the Abertillery constabulary. Two of the detectives, Detective Chief Superintendent Albert Helden and Detective Sergeant Alfred Soden were regarded at that time as two of the most famous crime fighters in the land. Helden alone, in his thirty year police career had solved twenty murders and countless other serious crimes which had sent a number of felons to the gallows.

Queen Street School, Abertillery. Freda had attended this school the day before her murder. On the left is Detective Sergeant Alfred Soden and on the right is Detective Chief Superintendent Albert Helden. Freda was seen by a witness near the gas lamp shortly before she disappeared.

Detective Sergeant William McBride had accompanied Helden and Soden to Abertillery to take photographs of the crime scene. For days they searched a barn fifty yards away from the lane where Freda's body was found, convinced that this was the murder scene. On the floor of the barn was a pile of chaff that had an impression in it of someone having been laid down and Freda's body had been found covered in chaff. Outside the barn there were footprints in the soft mud leading to the lane. It was some time before it became apparent that the barn was in no way connected to her death.

The Old Barn (circled) with X marking the approximate area where Freda's body was found in the lane. Photograph circa 1950 courtesy of Glenys Lee.

117

What was established however was that sometime after her demise she had been placed in a Hessian sack which had contained particles of chaff and tipped out onto the lane where she had been discovered. Her body had then been placed lying parallel to and approximately eighteen inches away from the back garden wall of 19 Duke Street, with her hands and feet bound.

Freda's funeral was held on Thursday 10th February 1921 and an estimated 100,000 spectators lined the streets to Brynithel Cemetery where she was buried. Harold Jones himself dutifully attended. The same day the police were informed of a warehouse that Harold Jones' employer owned which was situated in the rear yard of 108 Princess Street, Abertillery. Upon searching it they found a handkerchief on the floor, which had been in Freda's pocket the morning she had disappeared.

Inside the warehouse, with the handkerchief on the floor (circled).

Here was the murder scene. In the warehouse they also found a wooden axe handle, which they believed had been used to cause an injury to Freda's forehead. The police were now sure that Freda was killed in the warehouse shortly after she had left the seed store about 375 yards away. They also believed that the killer had left her body in the warehouse until darkness fell and then carried it to the lane at the rear of Duke Street where it was found the following morning. Although the police suspected Harold Jones was Freda's killer they couldn't prove it. He had a cast iron alibi regarding his movements the morning Freda had gone missing. The owners of the seed store, Herbert and Rhoda Mortimer told the police it would have been impossible for Harold to have left the store, go to the warehouse, kill Freda and return without them being aware. Three of Jones' friends also told the police about their movements with Jones throughout the remaining part of the day and evening.

The Scotland Yard detectives returned to London on Saturday 19th February after twelve days of fruitless inquiries. Their departure was generally interpreted as a sign of failure in their efforts to apprehend the killer.

The inquest into the death of Freda began on 24th February 1921 when, after five adjournments, on 7th March the jury reached their verdict. After hearing evidence from Dr Thomas Baillie-Smith the MOH for Abertillery, the jury formally announced the following verdict: (1) *'That the cause of her death was shock consequent upon (a) rape or attempted rape and injuries to the vulva and hymen (b) injuries to the neck and partial strangulation (c) injuries to the forehead (d) nervous shock and fright (2) and do further say that a person or persons to the jurors unknown did connivingly, wilfully and of malice aforethought murder the said Freda Elsie Maud Burnell.'*

Hours before the jury's decision on 7th March, Harold Jones had been detained at Abertillery police station after evidence that had been given throughout the inquest appeared to implicate him in Freda's murder. Detectives Helden and Soden of Scotland Yard had returned to Abertillery and formally arrested Jones at Abertillery police station at 8.00pm on the evening of the final day of the inquest. He was remanded in custody until Tuesday 5th April when he then appeared at Abertillery Magistrates' Court.

Sir John Rolleston Lort-Williams KC undertook the case for the prosecution and Mr William J Everett was entrusted with the defence. Following a four day hearing the magistrates' chairman Mr WB Harrison announced to the court that a prima facie case had been made against Jones and that in the interests of justice, Jones would stand trial at the next Monmouth Assizes. Jones shouted out: *'I am not guilty; I have always said I am not guilty and I am still saying it.'* He was remanded in custody at Usk Prison.

Jones' trial began at Monmouth on Monday 20th June1921 and was heard before Mr Justice Bray and jury.

Sir Reginald More Bray 1842 – 1923. This photograph of a portrait of Sir Reginald was taken by his great grandson Tom Butler. The original portrait was donated to the Inner Temple of the Law Society by his great granddaughter Handa Bray.

Sir John Rolleston Lort-Williams KC and Mr Charles Francis Vachell KC undertook the case for the prosecution and the defence case was entrusted to Mr Joseph Bridges Matthews KC and Mr St John Gore Micklethwait.

Sir John Rolleston Lort-Williams 1881-1966. Photograph 1923 published by permission of the Worcestershire Archaeological Society. Source: Worcestershire Record Office.

Mr St John Gore Micklethwait 1870-1951. Photograph circa 1921 courtesy of Brian Micklethwait, a grandson of the above.

During the first two days of the trial, circumstantial evidence was presented to the jury which made it appear as though Jones may have committed the murder, but there was no hard evidence presented that connected him to the victim.

The prosecution's case was that, when Freda left the seed store Jones went after her, told her to go to Mortimer's warehouse at Princess Street where he would give her the 10lb bag of grit that she had requested. He then tried to rape her and upon failing in this attempt killed her and returned to the seed store. They believed that Jones had left Freda's body in the warehouse until sometime after 11.00pm on the night of the murder, then returned to it and took the child's body to the lane at the rear of Duke Street. But no one had seen Freda after she had left the seed store and no one had seen Jones near the warehouse in Princess Street when the murder was alleged to have taken place. (The prosecution believed that the Mortimers who had been downstairs in the living quarters of the store at the time of the killing had given false evidence to protect Jones whom they believed was innocent.)

On the third day of the trial the defence presented a number of character witnesses. The first was Jones' father Philip. He said that his son had always been a good boy in relation to sexual matters and that following the disappearance and murder of Freda, Harold had never given him the impression that he had anything on his mind.

Harold's mother Nellie aged thirty-four, told the court that it would have been impossible for her son to have left the house during the night to take the body from Mortimer's warehouse to put it in the lane. Harold's bedroom door scraped loudly on the oilcloth floor covering and if the door had opened during the night she would have heard it. She also said her son had always been a good boy regarding his behaviour towards little girls.

The Jones' lodger, William Ernest Greenway aged twenty-four told the court that sometime after 11.00pm on the night of Freda's disappearance he had returned to his lodgings at 10 Darran Road and Harold was already in the house. After he and Harold had discussed Freda's disappearance they both went upstairs and slept in the same bed and both remained in it until 11.45 the following morning. He said if Harold had got out of bed during the night to move the body of Freda from the warehouse he would certainly have been aware of it.

William Ernest Greenway 1897-1963 and Caroline Green-way née Lowman 1902-1982. Photograph 1950s courtesy of Sheila Jones, granddaughter of the above.

Walter Waters, Jones' headmaster at school told the court: *'The teachers who had him in their charge and myself, never found anything to complain of in regards to him. We all found him exemplary, respectful and of good moral character.'* Other character witnesses followed and all told the same story. Jones was angelic.

The following day, Thursday 23rd June the judge began his complicated one-hour summing up. He concluded by telling the jury that it was the responsibility of the Crown to prove their case beyond all reasonable doubt. They had to establish that at about 9.30am on Saturday 5th February 1921, Jones had left the seed store, gone to Mortimer's warehouse 375 yards away and murdered Freda. The jury retired at 3.45pm and returned at 5.08pm. They didn't believe the prosecution had proved their case beyond all reasonable doubt and returned a verdict of *'not guilty,'* with the jury foreman adding *'and that is the verdict of us all.'*

There was pandemonium in the courtroom and the judge warned all present that he would jail anyone who caused a demonstration. Jones was released and led to a local restaurant where he made a speech from the balcony which included the words: *'I thank you all. I do not hold a grudge against the people of Abertillery for the horrendous ordeal that I have been put through. Well it's all right now. How could it be otherwise? I have told them all along I didn't do it. I knew nothing of courts, but I know of the fairness of a British judge. Mr Justice Bray saw the innocence I had protested all along. I had nothing but the truth to stick to. It came as the greatest surprise in the world to me to know that she [Freda Burnell] was missing.'* Jones was treated like a hero and whisked back to Abertillery in a charabanc sporting two large flags. On his way home through the western valley, crowds lined the streets waving and cheering. He arrived in Abertillery to a tumultuous welcome, the people waving flags. He was carried shoulder high through the streets by his supporters with a brass band playing and was reportedly presented with a gold watch.

On his arrival back home at 10 Darran Road, the first to congratulate him on his acquittal was Arthur George Little of number 4. He greeted Jones with the words, *'Well done Harold, we knew you didn't do it.'*

Arthur George Little with his daughter Iris aged three.

The vast majority of the population of Abertillery was convinced that Jones was innocent, but not so Florence Irene Little, aged eleven, the daughter of Arthur George Little. Florence repeatedly taunted Jones that he had got away with the murder of her school friend Freda. Shortly after the acquittal, in front of Jones and a number of his friends, she spat out: *'I know you killed Freda.'* Jones smiled politely and pretended to ignore her. Her fate was now sealed.

A *'Sunday Chronicle'* writer made a comment about Jones' demeanour throughout his trial. He wrote: *'Throughout the recent trial he was a great psychological study, inasmuch as he could change one moment from a fierce attack, such as he made on the counsel who prosecuted him at Monmouth Assizes, to an attitude of absolute composure. His fighting demeanour in the witness box, when Vachell, KC, who prosecuted, brought to bear upon him all his legal skill and penetration, was a revelation to those who have spent years in the courts of law. No greater indication of his rapid changes of temperament could be given than in the scene with his mother after his acquittal. As she strained him to her breast the boy himself from laughter burst into tears, crying, "Mother, you make too much fuss," drawing away from her once more and bursting into laughter again.'*

A photograph of Jones taken shortly after his acquittal. The cost of reproducing this Associated Newspapers Ltd/Solo Syndication Ltd image sponsored by Shane Owens, Abertillery. Fifteen years experience in carpentry and property maintenance. All work undertaken. Tel. Mob: 07920440383.

The body of Florence Little being removed from 10 Darran Road. The cost of reproducing this Daily Mail/Solo Syndication photograph sponsored by Luke and Lauren Tetley, Abertillery.

Chapter 13

Another Outrage

On Saturday 9th July 1921 just sixteen days after Jones' acquittal of the murder of Freda Burnell, an air of astonishment gripped the Abertillery area. Masses of people out of work owing to the 1921 miners' strike were whipped up into a frenzy when it became common knowledge that Harold Jones had again been arrested. A crowd of around five hundred surrounded Abertillery police station threatening to kill the officers inside. They believed that because the police had been unable to secure the conviction of an innocent boy for the murder of Freda Burnell, they were prepared to victimise him instead. Their attitude soon changed however when Superintendent Henry Lewis stood on the steps of the police station and announced: *'I have found the body of the child in the attic of Harold Jones' house foully murdered and I have arrested Harold Jones. I think that is all I can tell you and you will help us please by dispersing and going to your homes.'*

The child referred to was the tormentor of Harold, eleven-year-old Florence Irene Little of 4 Darran Road, Abertillery, who had vanished the previous evening after playing with her seven-year-old sister Lillie May and some friends outside Harold Jones' house at 10 Darran Road.

Florence Irene Little. 13th February 1910 – 8th July 1921. This photograph taken at Queen Street School, Abertillery circa 1919 shows the striking resemblance between Florence Little and Freda Burnell. (see page115) The cost of reproducing this Associated Newspapers Ltd/ Solo Syndication Ltd image sponsored by Julia Milkins, Abertillery.

As with Freda Burnell, thousands had scoured the hills and mountains of Abertillery looking for Florence. Harold and his father Philip aged thirty-six, took the lead in the search, Harold brazenly suggesting to the police that they send to Cardiff for bloodhounds to assist. Harold, after *"searching"* for the child from around 10.45pm on the night of her disappearance until 3.30am the following morning then returned home and went to bed. So soundly did he sleep that at 8.00am he had to be awakened by his father by having his feet tickled. Soon after, Harold left the house and the police who had secretly kept the front and back of the premises under observation during the night entered and searched it. One of the officers, PC Wilfred Cox, noticed that the area around the attic had recently been cleaned.

PC No.2 Wilfred Cox (circled rear right) at the rear of Abertillery police station in 1923. Next to him is PC No.272 George Tucker and in the front row is Sergeant No.53 James Jones. All three officers were involved in the Freda Burnell murder inquiry.

Entering the attic he found the body of Florence draped over the rafters. Her throat had been cut and a shirt belonging to the Jones' lodger, William Ernest Greenway was found wrapped around her neck.

The attic where the body of Florence Little was discovered.

Jones' father searched for his son and brought him back to Darran Road where he vehemently denied knowing anything about how Florence came to be in the attic above his bedroom. He was arrested and taken to Abertillery police station and from there was whisked away to a secret destination. The police feared for Jones' life owing to the anger of the crowds who earlier had wished to kill the police but were now desirous of killing him. When he left the police station, crowds witnessed Jones as he sat as proud as a peacock in the back of the police vehicle, smirking as he brushed fluff off of his jacket.

Florence Little's funeral was held on Wednesday 13th July 1921 and over 100,000 people lined the two-mile route to Brynithel Cemetery.

The funeral procession leaving Darran Road. Florence's siblings, nine-year-old Cyril and seven-year-old Lillie May are walking directly behind the coffin. Photograph courtesy of Victor Penaluna, second cousin of Florence.

Jones who had had the gall to *"pay his respects"* at the funeral of his first victim Freda Burnell was at this point safely tucked away in prison. He was subjected to a number of remands and court appearances still loudly protesting his innocence.

Finally a date was set for him to stand trial at Monmouth Assizes for the murder of Florence Little; 1st November 1921.

Shire Hall Monmouth, the location of the Monmouth Assizes.

BOY FREED IN MURDER IS HELD FOR ANOTHER

Acquitted of Strangling Girl, Welsh Lad of 16 is Seized As a Second Girl's Slayer.

Copyright, 1921, by The New York Times Company.

Special Cable to THE NEW YORK TIMES.

LONDON, July 9.—A charge of murder in circumstances perhaps unprecedented in the history of crime was made today against Harold Jones, a 16-year-old lad of Abertillery, Wales.

Only sixteen days ago he was acquitted, after a long trial, of the murder of Freda Burnell, an 8-year-old child, who last February was found strangled in an outhouse of the shop where Jones was employed as an errand boy. The girl had been attacked.

Friday evening Flora Little, aged 11, was missing at bedtime. Her parents and their neighbors sought her all night among the mountains, Jones assisting in the search.

The police today went through Jones's house and found a trapdoor leading from Harold's bedroom to the attic space beneath the roof. Forcing the door up they discovered the body of the girl, her throat cut. Jones was arrested for her murder.

The story as reported in the New York Times

Philip Samuel Jones 1884-1956 and his wife Nellie Eleanor Jones née Stevens 1886-1965. This photograph was taken two weeks after the murder of Florence Little at 46 Under Houses, Rhiw Parc Road, Abertillery. The Jones family, minus Harold moved here immediately after the body of Florence Little was found in the attic at 10 Darran Road. © Mirrorpix.

To everyone's surprise, Jones who had protested his innocence now admitted that he had killed Florence.

```
                 To
                    W. J. EVERETT
                         SOLICITOR.  PONTYPOOL   Mon,.



                    I HEREBY  state that it is my intention   to
            -   plead guilty of the crime of having murdered Florence Little
                upon which I now stand charged

                         Dated this    19  day of October 1921

                                        Harold Jones.
```

Jones' letter to his solicitor stating his intention to plead guilty to the charge of murdering Florence Little.

The reason being his counsel Mr St John Gore Micklethwait had warned him that his life was in the balance. If he stuck to his *"not guilty"* plea and the case ran before a jury beyond 11th January 1922, Jones' 16th birthday and he was then found guilty of murder, he may hang.

Jones is here pictured at his trial. © Mirrorpix.

Mr Justice Roche, presiding, after accepting Jones' plea, ordered that he be detained at His Majesty's pleasure and he was led downstairs.

Sir Alexander Adair Roche (Baron Roche of Chadlington, Oxon) 1871-1966, seen here talking to "The Provost of All Souls" during a break at Oxford Assizes circa 1930. Photograph courtesy of Elfreda Wallace-Jones, granddaughter of Sir Alexander.

Mr Charles Francis Vachell prosecuting then asked Mr Justice Roche if he could read out a confession that Jones had made while in prison awaiting trial and he agreed. The statement read:

'I Harold Jones wilfully and deliberately murdered Freda Burnell in Mortimer's warehouse on 5th February 1921. I also do confess that I wilfully and deliberately murdered Florence Little on 8th July, causing her to die without preparation to meet God. The reason for doing so being the desire to kill. Flora was about to leave the house when I got hold of her, seized her and cut her throat with a knife in the back kitchen, putting her head over the wash. I then went into the front room, leaving Flora's body in the wash. I went into the kitchen, bringing a shirt, which I wrapped around her head. I carried the body upstairs, brought a little table out of the room, put the body on the table and then got on the table. I took the body in my arms and tried to push it up into the garret (the attic). I then replaced the body on the table and went downstairs to get a rope in the back yard.

I returned upstairs and tied the rope to the body. I got on the table and dragged myself through the manhole with the end of the rope in my hands. Then, finding the rope not long enough to get through the manhole, I got back on the table, tied my handkerchief to the rope, clambered up through the manhole, and dragged the body up to the loft. After getting back to the table I replaced the cover on the manhole, replaced the table in my room and went downstairs to get a bowl of water and a cloth. I took it upstairs to wash off the stains of blood on the walls, the landing and the table. I went downstairs to fetch a candle and finding more bloodstains, I washed them off. I went downstairs throwing the water out of the bowl into the 'bosh' [the sink]. Just as I was having a bath, Mrs Little came to the door-just as I was washing my head and my body. I denied Flora was in the house and went back and finished my bath. I hereby declare the above statement to be true.' It was signed Harold Jones.

Kitchen of Harold Jones' house. Note the "bosh" (sink) bottom right.

It transpired that when Florence had been playing outside Jones' house on the night of her murder, Jones used his own sister, nine-year-old Flossie to entice Florence into the house with a promise of a drink of lemonade. If Florence had genuinely believed that Jones had killed Freda Burnell she certainly had no fear for her safety on that occasion. A factor in her entering Jones' home may have been that it was a sweltering summer's evening and she was thirsty. When his sister Flossie left the house to visit an aunt nearby, Jones pounced and killed Florence. During the post-mortem on his victim it was discovered that only two teaspoons of blood remained in the body.

Shortly after Harold Jones' conviction, a number of regional, national and Sunday newspapers commented on Jones and the atrocities committed by him. On Saturday 5th November 1921 a writer with the '*World's Pictorial News*' wrote: '*According to Mr Justice Roche, overweening vanity and a desire to be in the public eye contributed to the mental perversion of Harold Jones, the fifteen-year-old Welsh boy who has confessed to two brutal crimes, under circumstances unsurpassed in criminal records. Guilty on his own confession of two of the most infamous murders in the criminal history of England, Harold Jones the Abertillery boy of fifteen years of age awaits the future at Usk Gaol with the same calm as he faced the court [four days previously]. This giant among boys is a master of cunning and a temperamental quick-change artiste of the most astonishing type…. He could banish what to others would be of the greatest concern like flicking dust from a sleeve…. It was a close study of these [literary as well as trashy detective stories] that enabled him to put up so good a fight against Scotland Yard so as to secure an acquittal on the first occasion. Jones was as vain as a peacock, although he knew he had nothing to hope for, as he was pleading guilty and doubly confessing. He made toilet preparations of theatrical detail, his hair was specially done, his collar was white and fitted nicely round his black and gold knitted tie which from its well designed knot, slipped straightly down into the waistcoat of his blue serge suit. Later, he threw an eye round the court packed with women of all ages, then sat down with his arms folded, like a matinée idol in a drawing-room scene at a West End theatre. The reason he was so calm lay in his vanity. He knew the great advantage of pleading guilty where he knew he had no chance of escaping his guilt. What had to be said about him he didn't mind. He knew, too, that he would not have to pay for his crime with his life…'*

Darran Road 1921. The girl top right on the front of number 10 (marked X) is Jones' sister, Flossie Eleanor Jones, 1st January 1912 – July 2001.

The 'News of the World', the 'Daily Mirror' and hundreds, if not thousands of newspapers worldwide covered the astonishing events that occurred in Abertillery between February and November 1921.

Shortly after his imprisonment Harold Jones from his prison cell, explained why he had committed those heinous crimes. He claimed in 'The Sunday Chronicle' that "voices" had told him to kill. He would have picked that old chestnut from one of the crime novels he read so eagerly. He went into great detail when gloating over how he had beaten the country's finest detectives from Scotland Yard during the Freda Burnell murder inquiry. Jones said that when Freda had left the seed store in Somerset Street, he chased after her, telling her to go to Mortimer's warehouse at Princess Street where he would catch up with her and give her the 10lb bag of poultry grit.

Mortimer's warehouse on the left, (with the galvanised roof) showing the doorway into the shed from the lane. Further up and left was where the body of Freda had been found.

Inside the warehouse showing two 10lb bags of poultry grit on the top shelf. Jones promised Freda one of these bags if she met him at the premises.

He didn't walk with her but followed from a safe distance with the sole intention of killing her. He then went into gruesome detail, bragging that it took him no longer than eight minutes to leave the shop, attempt to rape the poor child, kill her, and return to the seed store unnoticed. He said: '*The great secret of my success I believed, was to say nothing and confound, by my actions, anyone who could say that they saw me near the warehouse and with the girl. When evening came I carried out the plan I had worked out for the disposal of the body; this is where Scotland Yard went wrong. They thought that I had carried the body from the warehouse in the early hours of the morning. [Sunday] I put the body in the lane early Saturday evening. It was so light, so fragile, that I could easily carry it under one arm.*'

Jones bragged how at 10.30pm on the night of the murder, he had used three friends to provide him with an alibi that he could not have put the body in the lane prior to 10.30pm. (Which of course he had done.) He had asked them to take a walk with him to Mortimer's warehouse at Princess Street because suddenly it had occurred to him that he had forgotten to lock the door when he had gone there to fetch a bag of potatoes with the owner's son earlier in the day. When they reached the warehouse Jones pretended to lock the door and then all four boys walked up the lane, which was a shortcut to Jones' home. It is believed that Jones, who knew exactly where Freda's body lay, walked over it with slightly splayed legs. His three friends walked on in the dark without suspecting that they had furnished Jones with his craftily planned alibi. By the time they reached Jones' front door it was 11.00pm and they watched him safely into his house. His alibi was now watertight.

He said: '*Of course, I had it all clear then. I went home quite satisfied that I was safe, I slept, and did not dream. I asked after the missing girl, and felt not a qualm at the asking. I did not think of the crime, and decided to stick to the old detective story teaching of letting the hounds make the first move and not break cover until forced. The arrival of the Scotland Yard men fascinated me. I had only read of Scotland Yard men before. Now I saw them in the flesh and I beat them. Whenever I found them testing the weak spots in my case, I strengthened them until finally, as the result of the trial proved, the best detective minds in Britain could not break it down...*'

After Jones' trial on 1st November 1921 he was initially taken to Usk Prison where he was detained until 30th November when he was transferred to Dartmoor Prison. He remained at Dartmoor until February 1923 when he was then transferred to Maidstone Prison in Kent. Dr Norwood East the Senior Medical Officer at Brixton Prison London, wrote a medical report detailing a conversation that he had with Jones at Maidstone Prison on 31st October 1923. He observed that Jones showed no remorse whatsoever when talking about his victims or their families. Dr East said: '*I consider that he lacks an appreciation of the enormity of his crimes. For him the sexual act reaches its highest gratification when accompanied by cruelty.... That both murders were due to sadism.... That the case is probably complicated as is not infrequent with fetishism - handkerchief collecting - that the origin of this latter is connected with an association of early sex experience.*'

In 1936, fifteen years after he had been incarcerated, the governor of Maidstone Prison wrote a report on Jones. In part it read: '*Jones works very well, he is intelligent and very alert. I have had many talks with him and am convinced that his crimes cause him no worry. He is callous but would be the last to admit it. Sad as it may seem I can see no hopeful prospects for Jones in the future...*'

The report was signed B Grew, Governor. The prison chaplain also saw Jones as a "*no hoper"* The *"no hoper"* Jones was sent to Camp Hill Prison, Isle of Wight on 29th July 1940. On 29th September 1941 Alexander Henry Paterson, who had been appointed Commissioner of Prisons in 1922 wrote a four-part report on Jones with his release in view. Part four of the report reads: *'The war will give him his opportunity. If as "Harry Jones" he can be specially enlisted in the Royal Engineers, he will give good service and one day should be the father of happy children.'*

Paterson, later Sir Alexander Henry Paterson had the desire always to look for the good in a person. While his motive was noble, in reality disastrous results can and do often ensue with murderers released from prison killing again.

Another prison *"do-gooder"* who was best known for his eccentricity was Lord Longford who died in 2001. He had spoken openly of his belief that moors murderer Myra Hindley who had been described by the press as *"the most evil woman in Britain"* and who had been involved in the murders of five children, had repented of her sins. Longford's bid to get Hindley released failed and she died in prison in 2002 aged sixty. Before she died she admitted that her plea for parole based on repentance was: *"on the whole, a pack of lies."*

(It was a great pity that Longford didn't live long enough to hear Hindley acknowledge that she had made a fool of him!)

Part three of Dr Norwood East's report on Jones in 1923 states: *'The murders [of Freda Burnell and Florence Little] were not the result of a disassociation or unconscious motive, but of a conscious aim; that consequently psycho-analysis with its present uncertainties is not indicated and would probably be foredoomed to failure, in that for success, the willing co-operation of the patient and desire for cure is essential. The prisoner however shows no remorse for the crimes and no apparent desire for any alteration in his condition.*

In view of the fact that psycho-analysed patients are being received into prison after failure of this treatment, a false sense of security and idea of a cure might result from a course of treatment, the efficiency of which could only be determined by the enormously hazardous experiment of releasing the prisoner.'

The beginning of the *"enormously hazardous experiment"* was carried out on 20th November 1941 when Jones was transferred to Wandsworth Prison, London, from where he was released onto an unsuspecting public on 7th December 1941. (See Jack of Spades on front cover. The mugshot of Jones was taken the day before his release. Photograph courtesy of The National Archives.)

Extreme pressure to release Jones had been exerted by Alexander Henry Paterson with total disregard for the reports of prison governors, psychiatrists and psychologists. Paterson haughtily believed he knew better than anyone else. (Born in 1884, Paterson died in 1947 soon after he had received his knighthood.)

Jones had been released into the temporary care of an aunt in Slough, Berkshire. A detective with the London Metropolitan Police Homicide and Serious Crime Command Review Team has informed the author that Jones *did not* enter the armed forces after his release from prison. (It seems unlikely that Jones would have been a willing participant in warfare bearing in mind that he cried like a baby whenever he was spoken to sharply while in prison.) Owing to the war years and the suspension of the electoral roll his place of residence cannot be traced between his release and 1947.

Peter Karrie, star of television, radio and stage, who wrote the foreword for the book *"Every Mother's Nightmare - Abertillery in Mourning,"* believes that Harold Jones had been born with an evil gene in his brain and probably died with that gene still in attendance.

Peter, best known for his portrayal of the lead role in Sir Andrew Lloyd Webber's musical *"Phantom of the Opera,"* ponders the question: *'Were there other incidents attributable to Harold Jones?'* Peter is not alone. There are many, including members of Jones' own family who are convinced he committed other atrocities after leaving prison.

The author believes Jones was involved with the Hammersmith nudes' murders for a number of reasons. He was released from prison because it was hoped it would give him his chance in life. The fact that Jones was seen as a *"no hoper"* by the prison authorities just five years before his release didn't seem to have any bearing on it. Jones told the authorities that he had no wish to be free from the desire to kill, so it would seem logical that given the opportunity to kill again, he would. He was in the Hammersmith district during the time of all the nudes' murders, using various names. It was discovered in 1921 that Jones had a fetish for collecting things that no normal person would wish to collect.

The Manchester newspaper *'Thomsons Weekly News'* in its Saturday 12th November 1921 edition stated:

'Another thing which has moved the authorities to keep the boy under observation is that before his arrest he had developed strange ideas, which are only observable as a rule, in very old people…. A fixed idea would make him collect things which no one in his sober senses would dream of keeping and this and other conditions brought about a morbid state of mind….'

The night he murdered Florence Little, Jones had been carrying in his pockets seven ladies handkerchiefs. Charles Francis Vachell who prosecuted Jones for the murder of Florence Little, told Mr Justice Roche that he believed, regarding the handkerchiefs, *'there may have been some perverted lust playing a part in the deed'* (the murder of Florence). The Senior Medical Officer of Brixton Prison, Dr Norwood East who had a lengthy conversation with Jones on 31st October 1923, also came to the conclusion that there was a sinister motive for Jones carrying the handkerchiefs.

Did the removing of teeth and/or clothing from the eight murdered prostitutes between 1959 and 1965 have a bearing on a perverted lust playing a part in these murders? The police at the time believed that the killer had removed the teeth and clothing to stop the victims from being identified. This seems a very unlikely reason as one after another all the victims were quickly identified. A more likely reason for removing the clothing, the teeth, and other possessions would be to keep them as trophies. Did the childlike stature of all eight west London victims have a bearing on their deaths?

On 7th July 2009, Stewart Evans, a former police officer who had joined the police force in 1969 contacted the author. Stewart, an acclaimed author of a number of the 1888 *"Jack the Ripper"* mysteries, said that he had always had a deep interest in the Hammersmith nudes' murders. He provided copies of old newspapers and magazines dealing with the subject. A most interesting article appeared in an undated colour magazine penned by renowned psychiatrist Dr James A Brussel. (The Sherlock Holmes of Greenwich Village, USA.) In his lengthy article Dr Brussel described his theory in detail on the Hammersmith killer whose crimes horrified Britain. In part he states: *'To begin with there is no doubt that he suffers from (or suffered, if he is dead) a severe mental disease, a psychosis. Schizophrenia is the most common psychosis, and is characterised by progressive mental deterioration – split personality. One type of schizophrenia is paranoid…. The paranoid has a mind that is sharp as a razor. Certainly the man who committed the Nude Murders had a keen mind; he has outwitted a great police agency. He is extremely precise, orderly, neat and cautious. He plans, not only the entire campaign of crime, he provides for all possible unexpected snags and obstacles. I feel our criminal had at least secondary school education. I feel he researched on his crimes; for example he went to the library and read such felonies as those of Jack the Ripper....'*

Although Dr Brussel's description of a paranoid schizophrenic would fit a number of people, it certainly appears to categorise Harold Jones. He had researched his *"cheap and trashy"* detective stories for years before his imprisonment and he most certainly continued to read these during his twenty years in prison and after his release. With the aid of these *"cheap and trashy"* detective stories and by using Mungo Ireland as his pawn had he beaten Scotland Yard again?

THE END

(See addendum on following pages.)

Addendum

O n 2nd June 2008, I received the following letter from Paul Rogers, a member of SCD1 – Homicide and Serious Crime Command at New Scotland Yard.

> '*Dear Neil*
> *Thank you for the copy of your book [Every Mother's Nightmare] and your kind words inside the front cover. The high quality of the finished article is a reflection of the enormous hard work, dedication and care you have taken to compile the sad facts of this case that you have skilfully managed to present in a sensitive yet entertaining way. The photographs you managed to collate were of great quality and really helped to set the scene. Congratulations on a great book, I look forward to your next project.*
> *Best wishes.*
> *Paul*'

Shortly after the launch of '*Every Mother's Nightmare – Abertillery in Mourning*,' I received a phone call from a woman who said that she had had the shock of her life after reading the book, only to find that Harold Jones was her mother's brother. Her husband had known for over forty years about Jones but had kept quiet about it. I have become friendly with this lady and her family and although it is not her fault what her uncle did, she does not wish to be identified. She took the book to her mother and asked her to read it. This was met with the reply: '*No thanks. There are enough skeletons in my family cupboard!*'

Since 2006, I have met many members of Jones' family who have shown extreme kindness to me or at the very least, politeness.

On 8th November 2008, a double page feature appeared in the '*Daily Express*' and the '*International Express*' linking Harold Jones with the murder of eleven-year-old Swansea schoolgirl Muriel Drinkwater in 1946. Other national, regional and local newspapers and radio stations took up the story. After giving it careful consideration and fearing that Jones' daughter may find out the truth about her father's past from the media, the following letter was written to her on 10th September 2009:

> '*It is with the greatest anxiety that I am contacting you. The reason I am doing so is because I have written a book which was published in May 2008. It is a True Crime story that is based on events that took place in my home town of Abertillery in 1921. My anxious concern is whether or not you are aware that the subject of the book is your father, Harold Jones/Harry Stevens/Harry Jones. If you are aware, then I would like to assure you that your identity and address are only known to me and the police. If you are not aware I can only apologise and tell you that, as national and international newspapers are reporting on my book, you may have a greater shock if you learned it from them.*
> *I have had contact with numerous members of your father's family in Abertillery and they have been very kind to me. I don't know if you are aware but your father had three sisters in Abertillery: Flossie born in 1912, ******* in 1924 and Constance in 1927. He also*

had a brother, Philip born in 1922. Only ******* is still alive... I have given long and careful consideration to writing you this letter and feel that owing to the enormous publicity given the book it would be for the best. I have known for the past eighteen months where you live but now realise that if you were unaware of my books existence you may find out in time.... I sincerely hope this letter doesn't cause you distress.'

On March 10th 2010, an email was received which was drafted by the sender on 13th November 2009. It obviously took a lot of thought over a four month period and a lot of courage to send it.

'Hi Neil.

I am sorry I have not contacted you after you writing to me about my father. I am still trying to come to terms with the whole thing. It was a great shock to find [my] father was a murderer (the man I knew as the most loving family man). I really need to read this book but unfortunately have not been able to obtain a copy. As I said I am still coming to terms with the whole thing. I will [contact] you when I feel able to do so without getting as upset as I am at this moment. I will tell you about the man (my dad) that I knew and the great father he was as I know it. The man I knew, that, you may find it hard to believe, a loving husband and father.'

As can be seen from my above letter to Jones' daughter, there is no mention of what Harold Jones had done in Abertillery in 1921. She found out from the many stories on the Internet.

Many emails have gone back and forth since March 2010, with Jones' daughter now aware of my suspicions that her father had been involved in other serious criminal activity since his release from prison in 1941. Jones' daughter who lives, let's just say somewhere in Bridgnorth, Shropshire is married and as far as it is known has no children.

I visited Jones' daughter and her husband in January 2011. I was treated kindly and hospitably which was a great relief not knowing how they would react to me. We still keep in regular contact.

I have also kept in regular contact with the Cold Case detective at New Scotland Yard who investigated Jones' possible connection to unsolved murders in England and Wales (see page 104). The following was received from him on 8th September 2009:

'Neil.

Thank you for taking the time to keep in touch. It's great to hear things are going well with your new book. Please let me know as soon as it is published as I will be keen to get hold of a copy. I think the Harold Jones story would make a great screenplay and hope you get the recognition that you deserve for all your hard work when it comes to fruition. It is the human story of the families and the community and the impact upon their lives that would certainly attract me to the re-telling of such a tragic case – I always think it is interesting to let the public know that these shocking crimes are nothing new. Your detailed research will certainly have taken a lot of hard work out of any such production.

Keep up all the good work.

Paul'

In July 2010, Frank Quinn, the son of 7th nudes' murder victim Frances Brown met author and broadcaster Professor David Wilson for a two hour discussion at Covent Garden, London. Frank told Professor Wilson, Britain's top criminologist and criminal profiler that he was convinced Harold Jones had murdered his mother. Frank had taken along to the meeting a copy of *'Every Mother's Nightmare – Abertillery in Mourning'* and presented it as a gift to Professor Wilson. Sky News producer Harriet Tolputt was also at the meeting and the plan was, to film a three minute short package dealing with the Hammersmith murders with Frank explaining how his mother's murder had affected him. The Sky News broadcast was due to be aired in August 2010. Unfortunately, Frank became distressed and the filming was cancelled.

On August 27th 2010, I received the following email from Professor Wilson:

'Neil

I spoke with Kate Beal yesterday who is commissioned to produce an eight part series for the Crime and Investigation Channel called Fred Dinenage's Crime Stories – I am working on the series as a presenter. I have explained about your book, Harold Jones and your new book about the Jack the Stripper murders. Kate wants to include all of this as an episode of the series – interviewing you about your work. I have copied Kate into this email so that she can make contact with you and explain more – and I have suggested that you should liaise regarding the timing of the publication of your book so as to gain the maximum publicity.

All the best. David.'

The next day, the following email was received from Kate, the Managing Director of Talent South, the film company commissioned to make the series.

'Dear Neil,

Professor David Wilson recommended we speak with you regarding our new series: Fred Dinenage's Crime Stories. David is our presenter expert for the series we are making for the Crime and Investigation Network. There are eight programmes in the series – each one focussing on a 20th Century crime. Fred and David will re-trace the crime and hopefully shed new light on each one. Essentially, looking at a 20th century crime through a 21st Century lens. We are filming over the next few months and they will transmit from March 2011. David told me about the Harold Jones case and your Jack the Stripper theory. We are really keen for one of the episodes to be based around Jones, including you and your discoveries….

Kind Regards. Kate.'

Filming of the drama/documentary took place at various locations in the Abertillery district on 25th and 26th November 2010. Scenes were shot around Abertillery town, in the Metropole Theatre, Abertillery Museum, the Tabernacle Chapel and the Rolling Mill public house. Susan Lloyd, Florence Little's niece was interviewed as was a niece of Harold Jones.

Re-enactments were filmed in Southampton throughout December 2010 and January 2011 with Cameron Beale aged thirteen playing the young Harold Jones.

An experiment was carried out in the function room of the Rolling Mill, Abertillery on Friday 26th November 2010. Six volunteers took part in an identity parade. In the line-up were Abertillery residents – Lee Bowyer, Jane Wilson, Emma Smith, Jack Edwards, Daffyd Stevens and Chris Arnold. Professor Wilson invited Fred Dinenage to speculate as to who out of the six most likely had a criminal record and who most likely didn't have one. After carefully considering the six he concluded that Lee Bowyer didn't have a criminal record whilst Chris Arnold most likely did have one.

The line Up

Top Left - Lee Bowyer, Jane Wilson and Emma Smith.

Top right - Jack Edwards and Daffyd Stevens.

Left - Chris Arnold.

Left to right. Professor David Wilson, Neil Milkins, Fred Dinenage MBE.

Professor Wilson then pointed out to Fred that the experiment proved how wrong one can be when trying to decide the guilt or innocence of a person without knowing the full facts. The majority of the people in Abertillery initially refused to believe that Jones had killed Freda Burnell based on his youthful looks and his mild-mannered outward behaviour. (Chris Arnold aged sixty-three is actually a former police officer with twenty-seven years service and had received the British Empire Medal from the Queen in 1992. Lee Bowyer did have a criminal record as he had been prosecuted for smoking whilst a teenager.)

Professor Wilson gave his opinion that Alexander Henry Paterson; the Commissioner of Prisons had acted foolishly when ignoring the advice of prison governors, psychiatrists and psychologists when he had pushed for Jones' release from prison. This would never be allowed today in British prisons. If a person convicted of child murder refused to co-operate with the prison authorities he would stay incarcerated until the day he died.

Professor Wilson stated that he believed it possible that Paterson's actions may have led to Jones becoming involved in many unsolved murders after his release from prison. He also commented on a homosexual relationship that Jones appeared to have been involved in while in Maidstone Prison. Jones and a prisoner with the surname Hewitt were known as the Romeo and Juliet of the prison.

Jones may have become involved in many unsolved murders!

Please consider the following:

(1)   At 10.45pm on Sunday 15th August 1965 Mr Ignac Ulycz a thirty-nine-year-old Ukrainian was fatally stabbed outside his own front gate at 323 Upper Richmond Road, Putney. He had earlier been drinking in the Northumberland Arms public house nearby. Just minutes before the stabbing his wife Maddalena had seen her husband approach the front gate of their matrimonial home from her window. As the killer had approached the Ulycz' garden gate at the same time as the victim, but from a different direction, Maddalena had heard her husband shout to the stranger: *'Get out of here.'* Mr Ulycz who was known to his friends as George, told Maddalena before he died that his assailant had done, said, or suggested something offensive to him. Was Ulycz stabbed because he had rejected the homosexual advances of the assailant? Maddalena told the police that the attacker was aged between fifty and sixty. (Jones was fifty-nine.) Another witness said that the attacker had run about half a mile from the scene of the crime, turned off Upper Richmond Road into Colinette Road and just seemed to vanish into thin air. (Jones lived at 20 Colinette Road. See map of Colinette Road and Upper Richmond Road on page107.)

The Wandsworth Boro' News of Friday 24th September 1965 reported on the inquest into the death of Ignac Ulycz. The first paragraph of the newspaper article stated: *'The man who killed Mr Ignac (George) Ulycz outside his home in Upper Richmond Road, Putney, may have been insane or a psychopath "who every now and then feels the desire to attack someone in this way," suggests the coroner, Mr Gavin Thurston at Fridays [17th September 1965] inquest.'* (If only the police had been aware that a psychopath going under the name of Harry Stevens was living at 20 Colinette Road, Putney at the time of the murder!) Jones vacated Colinette Road, Putney shortly after Ulycz' murder, moved to Hammersmith and changed his name from Harry Stevens to Harry Jones! Maddalena and her son Michael who was aged seventeen at the time of the murder never received justice. The jury at the inquest into the death of Ignac Ulycz returned a verdict that he had been murdered by *'a person unknown.'* George Ulycz' widow moved from Putney to Ringford Road, Wandsworth. She died in a care home in Watford in 2000. George Ulycz' son Michael who was seventeen at the time of his father's murder was very badly traumatised. He is married and lives in North Wales. He has a son Nick, who is Head of Global Research at HSBC Bank, London. He has been researching his grandfather's murder since the beginning of 2010.

(2)   Violet McGrath aged sixty-four. On Sunday 9th May 1954 at Onslow Square, Kensington she was hit with a blunt instrument and strangled with her own *stocking*. Distance from Jones house at Fulham? – three miles!

(3)   Muriel Maitland a mother of two was found murdered on 30th April 1957 in Cranford Woods near Heathrow Airport. She had been raped, her front teeth were smashed (like the nudes' victims!) and she had been suffocated and strangled. (Like Freda Burnell!) Distance from Jones' house at Fulham? – twelve miles.

(4)   On 24th May 1957 Teresa Lubienska a Polish countess aged seventy-three had travelled from Ealing Common to Gloucester Road tube station. Minutes after passing through Hammersmith she disembarked at Gloucester Road. Unseen by anyone she was stabbed five times in the chest on the eastbound Piccadilly line platform and died shortly afterwards. Nudes' murders investigator John du Rose – (*"Four Day Johnny"*) interviewed over 20,000 people during the Lubienska murder inquiry. The case is still unsolved. Distance from Jones' home at Fulham? Less than three miles.

There are striking similarities between this murder and a similar attack in Abertillery in November 1920. Mrs Minnie Louisa Higgins of 31 Heolgerrig was stabbed in the back as she entered her front gate. She screamed and her attacker fled into the darkness. He was never identified but many people in Abertillery cast their minds back to that night after Freda Burnell was found murdered. Was Minnie's and Freda's attacker the same person? After Jones' arrest for Freda's murder it seemed likely that they were. Out through Jones' back gate was the front of Heolgerrig!

When the one hour television documentary is aired throughout Britain and Europe in 2011, it is hoped that fresh information will be supplied by members of the public which will lead to the *"smoking gun"* regarding Harold Jones' involvement in the Hammersmith nudes' murders and others. If it does, it will be ironic that the person primarily responsible for identifying Harold Jones as the culprit was – Harold Jones! (see page 106).

Professor David Wilson in his interview with Fred Dinenage talked extensively about Harold Jones and his fetishes. In an email received from Professor Wilson on 29th November 2010, he states: *'Jones had an oral fetish – as is obvious from his desire to have someone spit in his mouth [that someone was Lena Mortimer, the thirteen-year-old daughter of Herbert Henry Mortimer, the seed store owner] and his collection of handkerchiefs. It seems to me significant that Jack the Stripper also took teeth from the mouths of his victims. To me this seems like part of an oral fetish too (as well as the teeth being a trophy). The key issue is that Jones and his fantasies would have developed from what they were like when he was a fifteen-year-old boy and therefore would not have been exactly the same – we all change over a long period of time. So, when he is fifteen he collects handkerchiefs, but when he is in his fifties he takes teeth.'*

On Wednesday September 8th 2010, the following email was received:

'Hi. I found some information online about a year ago that says you were due to release a book linking Harold Jones to the Hammersmith nudes' murders (and Mungo Ireland). Was the book ever released? I can't seem to find the name of it (in order to buy a copy).

My granddad was Mungo Ireland and I have been very interested in the case since his name was thrown up a few years back. Regards, S....'

I replied the same day: *'The book is due out in April 2011.... I have been researching for a long time the possibility that Mungo wasn't the killer but was implicated in the murders by Harold Jones. Would you speak to me on the phone? If so please email me your phone number.'*

The back garden of Jones' house. James Pope is sitting in his front garden at Heolgerrig in 1921. Just a short distance away at 31 Heolgerrig was where the unsolved stabbing of Minnie Higgins took place.

On Friday September 10th 2010, the reply came back:

'Thanks for the info Neil and thanks for the response.... Mungo was my dad's dad. Our family only got to know about my granddad's links to all this a few years back when a television channel got in touch with my nan [Elizabeth Ireland] who still lived in Putney at the time [132 Tildesley Road, Ashburton Estate, West Putney] where my dad grew up with his dad and mum [Mungo and Elizabeth] and four sisters back in those days. Nan's still alive but has since moved. She was contacted just after having a heart by-pass operation and when they said they were contacting her about it, of course it came as a bit of a shock to her, almost lethal I'd say. I must say that because of things like that I do feel reluctant to give information about my family members, but, that's how we all came to

hear of this. I am of course very interested in the case though, and especially the theory you have that my granddad was linked to Harold Jones, who is known to have been a murderer, apart from them living in the same area at the time. I will tell you that my dad has said he really doubts my granddad was capable of something like that (as do my aunties) though he did work on the Heron Trading Estate and he did work nights with access to the place where the bodies might have been [were] stored, he did commit suicide without any warning (although warnings are rarely given in such circumstances eh!) He was in the navy but I have never heard he was in the police force (as I have read).... If it's possible, can you enlighten me a bit more on the Harold Jones links and an idea of what some of your theories are – perhaps we could have a chat.......

Thanks, S....'

I have had extensive contact with the families of Mungo Ireland and his brother *"Harry"* since September 2010. I have put my cards on the table with them and told them that when I first started researching the Hammersmith nudes' murders, I was convinced that Harold Jones was the killer. As my research progressed I believed that Ireland and Jones had worked together as a tag team. I have told the Ireland family that my gut feeling now is that when Mungo Ireland committed suicide, Jones read about the incident in the local paper (it was reported on) and seeing a way to take the heat off himself contacted the police anonymously accusing Ireland of being the killer. Jones may also possibly have read a local newspaper story or heard by other means about Ireland being attacked on the Heron Trading Estate in the early hours of 18th October 1964.

Ireland had started his job with Night Security on 6th October 1964 and worked for them for less than three weeks when he resigned (or was fired), on 18th October. It is difficult to imagine how he could possibly have arranged for himself to be assigned to patrol the Heron Trading Estate. It seems probable or at least possible that as the Heron Trading Estate was almost nine miles away from Ireland's home at Putney, he had never even been to the estate prior to October 6th 1964. Helene Barthelemy's and Mary Fleming's bodies had been stored in the disused electricity transformer building on the Heron Trading Estate in April and July 1964 respectively, three – four months before Ireland took on his patrol job. It is known for sure that Harold Jones moved from the area where Ireland had lived shortly after the suicide and moved *four miles* away to Hammersmith changing his name again from *"Harry Stevens"* to *"Harry Jones."* He had moved to just two streets away from where 7th victim Frances Brown had lived and two streets away from where 8th victim Bridget O'Hara had lived. **Why!**

Finally, it is known that all eight nudes' murder victims were killed at different locations to where their bodies were dumped in various areas of London. It is also known that at least the last four victims had been stored in the electricity transformer shed on the Heron Trading Estate. Victims five, six, and seven were later dumped miles away from the estate. However, the eighth victim's body (Bridget O'Hara) had been deliberately camouflaged on the estate in a way that the killer knew (and wanted) it to be found. If Mungo Ireland had been the killer would it make sense for him to leave the body where even a fool would realise that as a previous worker at the estate, suspicion would be cast on him?

Acknowledgements

The author would like to thank the following for their help in compiling this book: Mr Ian Stephens, Head of Art, Abertillery Comprehensive School – Mrs Sian Burns, Head of Art, Brynmawr Foundation School – Hazel Cook, Local Studies Department, Kensington Central Library – Dr Jonathan Oates, Ealing Local History Centre – The National Archives, Kew, London – Anne Wheeldon and Jane Kimber, Hammersmith and Fulham Archives and Local History Centre – Margaret Towkatch and Shirley O'Mahony, Hammersmith and Fulham Cemeteries Dept. – London Metropolitan Archives – David Capus, Metropolitan Police Records Management – George and Maggie Bird, Metropolitan Police Service, Historical Collection – Adrian Lee, Daily Express – Greg Burns, Fulham and Hammersmith Chronicle – Kensington and Chelsea Chronicle – Westminster Chronicle – Dominic Jones, Gwent Gazette – Mike Buckingham and Laura Evans, South Wales Argus – Nathan Bevan, Wales on Sunday – Aidan Jones, London Informer and Hounslow Chronicle – Steve Thomas, Barry Local Studies Library – Liverpool Record Office, Central Library Liverpool – V Jane Baxter, Local Studies Library, Richmond Surrey – Felix Lancashire, Wandsworth Heritage Service, Battersea Library – Tony Sharkey, Blackpool Central Library – Vicki Eltis, Surrey Herald – Antoinette Teasdale – Melissa Parry – Ian Britton – Kirsty Gibbins, East Lothian Courier – Dan Hodges, Ealing Gazette – Alison Bott and Jacqui Morley, Blackpool Gazette – Sharon Harris, Barry and District News – Elizabeth Lee, Northampton Chronicle and Echo – Ray Worsley, Blackpool – Irene Dimond, Barry – Joe Pignatiello, BBC Radio Northampton – Jim McBeth, Scottish Daily Mail – Chris Wickham, Richmond and Twickenham Times – Scott Hesketh, Daily Star Sunday – Frank and Gerry Marcangelo, Bridge Café Acton – Carolyn Hammond and James Marshall, Chiswick Local Studies Library – Richard Youngs, Archives and Special Collections, Glasgow – Sarah Calkin, Castle Point Echo (Essex) – National Library of Ireland – Chat magazine, (August 6-13 2009 issue) – Alan Rice, Chiswick (New) Cemetery (burial records) – Marcia Williams, Wandsworth Borough Council, (rates records) – Andrew Smart – Downs Mail, Maidstone – Dr John Thurston – Gavin Thurston – Dan Wainwright, Express and Star, (Stafford) – Rob Taylor, Black Country Bugle – Peter Newman, BRfm Radio, Brynmawr – Chris Jarvis, Venture Wales, Brynmawr – Bob Smyth, The Sunday Post (Scotland) – Arnold's Funeral Services, Bedford – Steve Jones, Welsh Development Agency – Sarah Wasley, Granta Books, London.

Special thanks to Fred Dinenage – Glenn Chandler – Professor Bernard Knight – Peter Karrie – Mike Spencer – Jon Nixey – John Edwards, Tillery Windows Cwmtillery – Samantha Otley, Pontypridd – Emma Harris, Abertysswg – Len and Kim Wilkes, Greenford – Nick Coombs – Neil Deacon – Gwent Police and Gwent Police Authority for permission to use a number of important photographs throughout this book – Blaenau Gwent County Borough Council and UK Steel Enterprise Limited – Louise Harris, Julian Bosley and Mohammed Forouzan, Economic Development Unit, Regeneration Division, Blaenau Gwent County Borough Council.

Extra special thanks to: Professor David Wilson – Paul Rogers, SCD1, Homicide and Serious Crime Command, Special Casework Investigations Team, New Scotland

Yard, London – Harold Kenneth and Mark Buchan Jones, Manchester – Kim Rees, (daughter of Gwynneth Rees) – Stephen Sloman, (son of Hannah Tailford) – Thomas James Barthelemy, (son of Helene Barthelemy) – Frank Quinn, (son of Frances Brown) – Carolina and Sarah Quinn, daughters of Paul Quinn – Susan Mills, (daughter of Freddie Mills) – The families of Mungo Ireland and Henry Johnstone Ireland – and finally to the many family members of Harold Jones who have shown understanding and extreme kindness to the author during research for this book.

Television Source –
Reggie Kray: The Final Word BBC1 29th March 2001
24 Hours BBC1 2nd April 1970
Book source –
Found Naked and Dead by Brian McConnell, New English Library, London, 1974
Jack of Jumps by David Seabrook, Granta 2006
Murder Was My Business by John du Rose, WH Allen 1971
The Trial of Stephen Ward by Ludovic Kennedy, Gollancz, 1964; Penguin, 1965

A large amount of information in chapter nine of this book dealing with the police investigation into the death of Freddie Mills, was gleaned from MEPO 2 / 10756 which is stored at the National Archives at Kew, London.

Newspaper information source –
Daily Express – The Kensington News and West London Times – The Star – The Times of London – Western Mail – News of the World – Barry and District News and Barry Herald – Liverpool Echo – Brentford and Chiswick Times – Middlesex Independent – Sunday Chronicle – World's Pictorial News – Thomsons Weekly News – Daily Mirror – Thames Valley Times – Richmond Herald – Richmond and Twickenham Times – Evening News (London) – Sunday Telegraph – Daily Telegraph – Daily Mail – Evening Standard – West London Observer – West Lancashire Evening Gazette – Putney and Roehampton Herald – South Western Star, (Putney) – Wandsworth Boro' News – Shepherds Bush Gazette and Hammersmith Post – Daily Telegraph and Morning Post – Fulham Chronicle – South London Advertiser – The Independent – South London Observer – South London Press – Acton Gazette and Post.

The author has tried to trace all copyright details but where this has not been possible and where any amendments are required, the publisher will be pleased to make any necessary arrangements at the earliest opportunity. For any errors or omissions which are unintentional, the author offers sincere apologies.

Index

A

B

C

D

E

F

G

H

I

J